14.80

D1602413

DANCE AROUND
THE SUN

Mary Little Bear Inkanish in 1950. (Gouache by Margaret LeFranc)

DANCE AROUND THE SUN

THE LIFE OF
MARY LITTLE BEAR INKANISH:
CHEYENNE

ALICE MARRIOTT

AND

CAROL K. RACHLIN

Thomas Y. Crowell Company   New York   Established 1834

Designed by Joy Chu

Manufactured in the United States of America

Library of Congress Cataloging in Publication Data

Marriott, Alice Lee, 1910–   Dance around the sun.

Bibliography: p.
Includes index.
1. Inkanish, Mary Little Bear.   2. Cheyenne
Indians—Biography.   3. Indians of North America—
Mixed bloods—Biography.   I. Rachlin, Carol K.,
joint author.   II. Title.
E99.C53M37   970'.004'97 [B]   77-1859
ISBN 0-690-01450-3

1   3   5   7   9   10   8   6   4   2

Dear Mama,

For too many years we talked about my writing your book. Always we were too busy living it to write. Now the time has come when other things can be put aside, and you can speak for yourself at last.

I hope the words will come through strong and clear like a Sun Dance song. I hope your life will show others how to live. Our young people are lost and confused, and they need your voice to set them on the way. Carol feels as I do about this, and she joins me in saying, "Hah-hoh Pivé!" *("Thanks. It is good!").*

Ahneece

ACKNOWLEDGMENTS

There are many people to be thanked for the existence of this book. First of all, of course, Mama herself, and Papa Jim Inkanish. After them, all the Cheyenne people we have known in Oklahoma and Montana, especially Clark Inkanish, Mama's grandson, who contributed many pictures and much information; the late Jesse Davis, Mama's great-nephew; and Mrs. Libby Hawkins and Mrs. Carol Cussen Hampton (Mrs. James Hampton), Papa's nieces, who lent photographs and gave freely of their time and knowledge. And last but not least, Mama and Papa's son, Joseph Inkanish, for much kindness during all the years that we knew him.

The Bureau of Indian Affairs and Arts and Crafts Board personnel gave much aid over the years, and we would like to include the late Rene d'Harnoncourt and the late Frederic H. Douglas among the many who made some of the events described in this book possible for Mama and for us.

The Reverend Father Peter John Powell, and the late Laurance D. Cone sat out Sun Dances and powwows with us, and shared their knowledge and endurance with us, as well as their friendship.

Jack Haley, of the Western History Division of Manuscripts, University of Oklahoma, got out all Stanley Vestal's photographs for us. He was always kind and considerate, and he deserves more credit than we can possibly give him.

Finally, for help in manuscript preparation and reading, Deborah Wyant, Helen Putnam, and Mary LaCoste came forward whenever they were needed. Mable Morrow gave us much technical advice on the role of Plains Indian women generally. And again, as often before, Lawanna Kent Brown was there when needed for library and newspaper references, typing, and all the other odd jobs that beset writers.

This book is based principally on Mama's memory. If history or fact be belied, so let them.

Oklahoma City, Oklahoma 1976
Alice Marriott
Carol K. Rachlin

CONTENTS

INTRODUCTION

Some people are born with the qualities that make legends. To this category belong Emma Goldman, the revolutionary, and Queen Victoria, who made her name synonymous with conformity. Other women achieve legendary status through accidents of fate and time, like the first Elizabeth of England and Tallulah Bankhead. And those of yet a third category become living legends through sheer survival. To this last group belong María Martinez, potter, of San Ildefonso Pueblo, and Mary Little Bear Inkanish, a Southern Cheyenne.

Not that these two women did not deserve any status that accrued to them. Both were superb craftswomen and both had in the highest degree the quality that speakers of English call charm and that journalists of the 1970's call charisma. Neither had in any way an easy life, but both took tragedy in stride and passed beyond it to smile again. Most of all, they were bridge people between old American Indian cultures and the life-ways of the non-Indians with whom they came in contact. In *María: The Potter of San Ildefonso,* Alice Marriott has written about one of these women—who, like Mary Little Bear, was in many ways as close to her as her own mother. Now we shall try to write about the other.

Mary Little Bear was born at a time when the West was in a state of change and confusion and the Bureau of Indian Affairs was in the same condition. The Indians clung to the past and were forced to accept the advancing Anglo pressure.

She never knew her father. He, with at least one partner, opened a trading post at Darlington Agency, Oklahoma Territory, in the late 1870's. He stayed just long enough to meet and marry (by tribal custom) Mary's mother, Little Bear Woman, also known as Stone Woman. He begat Mary and her sister, the last of her mother's five children, and departed. Some people told Mary, in later years, that her father was a French-Canadian whose name was Block.

There could be no question about Mary's mother and her position in the world. The daughter, niece, sister, and mother of Sun Dance priests, she had earned great honor as the Sacred Woman of the Sun Dance, and had served in that capacity four times. She was a holy woman, a *Mah-hee-yuna;* one who gave her life and her body for her people. She was as secure as it was possible for a Cheyenne woman in the late nineteenth century to be.

Why, then, did she choose a white man? By all Cheyenne conventions, she could have had her choice of any prominent Cheyenne. Was this the ultimate in self-sacrifice? And did she regret it, to the point where she accepted the fact that her daughter had been named *Vee-hay-kah* ("White Girl"), which was in itself a term of degradation, if not of abuse? We will never know the answers to these questions because she never told them to her daughter. Mary never had an adult Cheyenne name. She was always known by her childhood name, and finally she grew proud of it.

To those of us who knew Mary as a mature and later an old woman, she was the reincarnation of her mother. An aristocrat and autocrat, she ruled her family with a will of Bessemer steel. Poverty came her way, but her head remained high. Tragedy could not pull her down. And as she grew older, she remembered more and more of the old days and ways, and became more and more Cheyenne in her thought and her actions.

It was our good fortune to be with Mama during much of the remembering period, when she turned more and more to the old times and what they stood for. Sometimes we witnessed an exercise in total recall; sometimes the layers of one culture were overlaid by those of another, and could only be peeled away gradually; sometimes in this story memory will conflict with written history and descriptions of places and people.

Unfortunately, an anthropologist works one jump ahead of the undertaker. This time the undertaker caught up with us. There are

many questions that will never be answered. There are more specu-
lations in some matters than there are conclusions. But always there
is Mama, that indomitable four feet nine inches of will and courage,
bird-boned, bird-light more often than not, and a ruling force
whatever the circumstances.

One question that has plagued us has been whether to tell
Mary's story completely from her point of view, in the third person,
or switch abruptly to the first, when we come into her life. On the
whole, the first course seemed preferable. So we ask you, the readers, to remember that when we say one or the other was present at
a certain event, we were.

Alice first, because she was there first and longest. Carol's place
in Mama's life came later; as Carol once said, "Mama was already
the little queen when I met her." But Alice knew her in work and in
play, in sorrow and in fun, and that part of the story should be told
too.

The material for this book was gathered over a period of forty
years in bits and pieces as Mary told of incidents from her life. There
may be some confusion, such as the blending of her first school at
Darlington with her second school at the Seger Colony. Also, the
description of the first Sun Dance she remembered is more impres-
sionistic than strictly factual. But the events she observed there,
which affected her life, are real and true.

Where dialogue is used in the early part of this book, it is as
Mary remembered and repeated it. The memories of older Cheyenne
Indians are very sharp and clear on such points and can be trusted.
Later in the book, the dialogue is as we ourselves remember it.

Something more must be said about Mary and Jim. During the
years that Alice knew Mary and Jim, and the years that Carol knew
Mary, and the years to the present, after her death, we thought that
she had only two children, Joe and Josephine. We only learned that
Mary and Jim had four other children when we asked her grandson,
Clark Inkanish, for family pictures to illustrate this book. We made
every attempt to find out about these people. The surviving
members of the family could tell us very little.

So that the reader will have some idea about these four children
we are going to share our scant knowledge.

George was born November 6, 1900. He married Rene Downing and had a son named Garth, who, we believe, is living in California. George was killed in an automobile accident sometime prior to 1937, when Alice first went to work with Mary.

James, Jr., was born August 29, 1904, and married Alice Sadonka, a Kiowa Indian. We know nothing more about them.

Maudie was born August 26, 1907, and married Stanley Edge, a Caddo Indian from Fort Cobb, which is about twenty miles west of Anadarko. She attended her mother's funeral but did not sit with the family. She died in the early 1970's.

William was born on March 29, 1910, and we know nothing more about him.

A word must be said about Joe, the only child who stayed with Mary until her death. He was born August 28, 1902. He is still living in Oklahoma, confined to a hospital with a terminal illness. We are both very fond of Joe, and admired his love for and devotion to his mother during her last years. Also we are very grateful to Joe, and to his son Clark, who contributed much support and encouragement and helped us see Mary as a mother and grandmother.

Why Mary, in the latter part of her life, mentioned only Joe and Josephine we do not know and will never know. We decided to tell Mary's story the way she wanted it told. Our love and respect for her dictated our decision. Hah-hoh, Mama. Hah-hoh.

DANCE AROUND
THE SUN

I

◇◇

THE PLACE

Darlington, Oklahoma, is a state game farm now. There it lies in a bend of the Canadian River, not very far from Old Fort Reno. The Fort itself has become a Department of Agriculture experimental station, for animal husbandry and cultivation of range grasses, but traces of its former glory remain in the old parade square, with its fencing of barracks, officers' quarters, and post shops. Even the socket that held the flagpole is there, with its surrounding oval of cedar trees, on the west side of the parade ground. And west of the post proper is the cemetery; Ben Clark, greatest of all the Cheyenne scouts the Cavalry ever hired, is buried there—as are German prisoners of war who died in internment in World War II.

Not so at Darlington. All the old Indian Agency buildings are gone except two homes from 1870. Nothing remains to mark the campsite across the river, although sometimes as many as a thousand people gathered there for the midsummer Sun Dance.

On the south side of the river, where the camp used to be set, there is still a grove of trees: cottonwoods, elms, hackberries, chinaberries. At the water side, where Cheyenne children used to play, the trees are looped together with wild grapevines, but no one bothers to gather the grapes now, or the wild sand plums clustered on the sunny slopes above the river terrace. Wild-grape jelly and sand-plum butter are as good now as they were when the Agency ladies of Darlington gathered and preserved the fruit in the 1870's and 1880's, but it is easier in these years to whip down the four-lane highway to the nearest supermarket and buy preserves from the well-stocked shelves.

Darlington and Fort Reno have their places in frontier history, whatever changes have taken place in a century. At one time, just before the Civil War, Fort Reno was one of the chain of outposts that marked the frontier from Montana to the Big Bend of Texas. Battles were fought from Fort Reno, and the Buffalo Soldiers, the Ninth and Tenth Mounted Infantry regiments of Negro troops, rode out from Fort Reno to the Staked Plains to the west. George Armstrong Custer, Philip Sheridan, and William Tecumseh Sherman all served tours at Fort Reno.

The history of Darlington, on the contrary, was meant to be a history of peace. The Agency and School were established there after the Civil War, under President Ulysses S. Grant's "Quaker Peace" administration. The Indians were not to be subjugated, but drawn into the ways of civilization. That everything did not go according to plan was not the Quakers' fault. It was the will of God.

Out and beyond the river the short-grass plains rolled like the ocean whose bottom they had once been. The soil was sandy and shallow, held in place by the dense cover of native grasses. In some places the earth was stained blood-red with leaching hematite; in others bone-white strata of kaolin showed starkly. Streams crossed the plains, bordered, like the river, with trees, but in the open country there was little if any shade or shelter.

This was no country for farming, and the Agency employees, with wooded and hilly Ohio and Pennsylvania to remember, shook their heads over it. The Agency people were the only farmers for miles in any direction; the Cheyennes were horsemen and horse breeders, who would not turn their skills even to raising cattle. The Cheyenne men would hunt, or they would race their horses for what the Agency people thought were sinfully high stakes.

The Cheyenne women were endlessly busy; endlessly gossiping. They were fine craftswomen and their quillwork and beadwork brought good prices at the trading post and the Fort. Cheyenne women especially enjoyed craftwork because it was a social occupation, not a lonely one. They sat in groups, indoors or out, and twittered about their designs like birds. Cheyenne women were as proud of their handwork as of their chastity (for which they were noted among the other Plains tribes).

For some years there was only the sutler's store at the trading post where the women could sell quillwork or beadwork and buy more beads. But in the late 1870's, two young men, French-Canadians, came to Darlington from the East. The sand blowing along the dry riverbed did not bother them, although they were dismayed by the sparseness and expense of building materials, which had to be freighted in. They had come, they said, to open a trading post at Darlington. They had papers to the Agent to prove that they had the right.

Nobody thought the young men would stay long, even though they boasted that their families would see they had all the goods and supplies they needed. Boasting was good, to the Cheyennes. One way for a man to prove he was a man was to strike the drumhead, recite his war deeds, and then, as a final act of conviction, jerk off his breech clout and wave it high, evidence of manhood exposed for all to see. Few men had earned this right by doing extremely brave deeds in war, but any man could boast. So the young men might boast of their families' wealth as much as they liked.

One of them, named Block, married a Cheyenne woman. Her name was Little Bear Woman. Her uncle was a Sun Dance priest, and her three sons by a previous marriage were studying the ritual under him. Little Bear Woman had taken part in the Sun Dance three times. The Agency people did not approve of the Sun Dance. They said such relations as the Sun Dance required between leading men and a woman were sinful and could even be incestuous, and put Heaven out of reach of everyone who became a participant.

Little Bear Woman and her family had always held their heads high, and they continued to do so. In fact, Little Bear Woman had been known to say that the Christian Heaven didn't sound like a place she would want to go to, alive or dead. She was a Mah-hee-yuna—a woman who gave her life, mind, and body to benefit her people. This was her duty and her joy, and she was above whatever the Quakers or anyone else might say.

So she married Block, by tribal custom, and had two children— both girls—by him. Later he left Darlington and returned east. That was the custom of his tribe, he said.

His oldest daughter, born in 1877, was a plump, pretty child, and except for her gray-blue eyes looked entirely Cheyenne. The problem was what to name her. The Cheyennes traced their descent

through their mothers, but a child's name was at least supposed to
indicate the identification of the father's clan. All Block had ever
said was that he belonged to one of the Lost Tribes. He had never
named them.

So, until a better solution to the naming problem could be
reached, they named her Vee-hay-kah: "White Girl." It wasn't really a name, but it was better than nothing. An Agency employee
later named her Mary, and said she should take her mother's name,
Little Bear, and Mary Little Bear she became. Only teasing children
used her other name. There were plenty who would tease a half-
white child in those days.

She grew up in the camp across the river from Darlington
Agency. The people no longer had buffalo hides for tipis. Most of
the Cheyennes lived in white-wall tents, like those the soldiers
used. Those who could afford them had a pot-bellied Sibley stove
for heating and cooking, its pipe running at right angles through
the side wall of the tent, to let out the smoke of cottonwood fires.
The poorer people cut holes in the tent roofs and cooked in a fire
hole beneath, as the Cheyennes always had done when they lived in
tipis. A few prestigious families, whose women had kept the old
skill of tipi cutting, had white-to-brown canvas tipis, the color
darkening as smoke penetrated the fabric. These were very grand
dwellings, and it was in the canvas tipis that ceremonies were held,
that the old men smoked and talked, and that children were told
stories on winter evenings.

Afterward, Mary wondered how much she really remembered of
her own experience and how much she recalled from what her
mother told her. She couldn't have remembered her small night
cradle, for instance. The first month of her life she spent in a plain
rawhide tube, rigid enough to support her back but easily unlaced
for changing the soft sage and rabbit-fur pads between her legs and
under her buttocks. Little Bear Woman could lift the baby, cradle
and all, to her breast for feeding.

In that first month, while she was still in the cradle, Mary
learned not to cry. The smallest whimper brought a firm, gentle
hand—her mother's or her aunt's—across her face to silence her.
There was little to fear from a crying baby in those days, but the

time had been when a whole Cheyenne camp could be attacked and destroyed because a child's wailing was heard. All Cheyenne children of Mary's age learned not to cry.

After a few months, the small cradle was exchanged for a "big horseback" cradle with snowshoe-shaped bois d'arc supports and two strips of horsehide across the back so it could be hung from the pommel of the mother's saddle. This, Mary remembered well, for she kept it many years. Her aunt had made it for her. It had a big beaded canvas hood, lined with flowered calico. The beads were of pale, delicate colors, and they were very small, to fit a little girl. Mary's brothers were almost grown men, and their cradles had long ago been sold. Mary was like the beginning of a new family for her mother, and so her aunt made her a new cradle all her own. She did not have to use a passed-down one.

There were hourglass-shaped woman's designs on the cradle, made with pale blue and yellow, and darker red beads against the white background. Only special, favorite children had such cradles. Perhaps Mary's aunt wanted the little girl to feel that she was loved and wanted before she could know anything else.

For the first year of her life, sleeping in the big cradle, Mary wore no clothes except rabbit-fur diapers which could be thrown away when they were soiled. She was wrapped in old worn blankets, washed soft. Little Bear Woman washed the blankets often and always had a supply of clean ones on hand.

At the Sun Dance, when Mary was about a year old, her aunt had a give-away in her honor. She had made Mary a pair of full-beaded moccasins—even the soles were beaded—to show that this little girl's family would not let her feet touch the ground if they could help it. And the aunt made Mary her first dress, exactly like a grown woman's calico dress. It was all cut from one piece of cloth, with a slit cut across for a neck opening. There was a braided yarn sash around her waist, tied at the left hip. There in the center of the Sun Dance circle, Mary's aunt lifted the child from her cradle and held her high, for everyone to see.

"Shell Woman, come here," she called. "This child wants to ask you a favor and give you a gift."

Later Mary was told that Shell Woman was old, old. She had fought like a man beside her man at the Sand Creek Massacre, and had killed four soldiers with her skinning knife. She could tell her war deeds as a man could, and for this reason people always honored and respected her as long as she lived.

Mary's aunt took from the hood of the big cradle the beaded turtle-shaped case that held a piece of Mary's navel cord. She held the ornament high, so everyone could see it too, and then handed it to Shell Woman.

"This is the other half of this child," Shell Woman said. "It came into this world when she did, and they should never be separated." She threaded the loop at the top of the case into Mary's sash.

"For almost a year this child and her mother were one, and for another year she has lived from her mother's milk," Shell Woman went on. "Now the time has come for them to become two people, each one whole and complete." She took her sewing awl from the case that hung over her right hip, and raised it above Mary's face. Quick as a flash, Shell Woman pierced one of the child's earlobes and then the other, and just as quickly she thrust a small, sharpened stick through each opening. "I have no name to give you, little one," Shell Woman said. "There will be many, many more like you in the years to come. For now, you shall be known as the White Girl, Vee-hay-kah, but you shall be loved by your people."

The family laid gifts before Shell Woman, even though she had not really given Mary a name. After all, it was a great honor that she had pierced the baby's ears. So they gave her the best they had: rawhide envelope-cases filled with dried meat, and hanks of beads and slabs of sinew, and even a new black silk head scarf and two new store blankets.

It was a fine give-away, and Mary's mother never let her forget about it.

"You are a Cheyenne and not a Cheyenne," she said once. "But remember this. When you were first shown to the people, you had the best we, your Cheyenne family, could give you."

2

❖❖❖❖❖❖❖❖❖❖❖❖❖❖❖❖❖❖❖❖❖❖❖❖❖❖❖❖

GROWING UP

The camp across the river from the Agency was as permanent as a Cheyenne camp could be. There were frames for brush arbors for summer, and there were brush windbreaks around the tents and tipis. In the old days, when camps were shifted every week or so, there would have been latrine areas laid out to the north and west, downwind except in the worst storms. Here the Agent insisted on wooden privies, like those the Agency's people used; the holes were dug deep, but the privies could be moved when necessary. And the privies, too, were downwind from the main camp.

South of the main camp were the sweat lodges. Every family had one of its own, or one that was shared with relatives. Here, too, changes showed. Once the sweat lodges would have been covered with buffalo hides, but now they were covered with canvas and brush, and, sometimes, old blankets. They looked poor and shabby to the older people, but to the young ones, who had never seen the old lodges, these looked like sweat lodges—that was all.

Mary had her first sweat bath when she was six. Her mother took her into the lodge. They took off all their clothes, and waited until Mary's half-brothers rolled hot stones through the small east door of the lodge. Little Bear Woman pushed the stones into a hole in the middle of the floor, and threw water on them from a tin bucket. The steam rose and filled the lodge, and Little Bear Woman showed Mary how to scrub and beat herself with branches of wild sage, and get clean all over.

"You must learn how to do this now," Little Bear Woman said, "because you will have to do it many times—at least once a

month—after you are a grown woman. Whenever there is a ceremony, or something important is going to happen to you, you
should take a sweat bath. If you are going on a long trip, this is the
thing to do. You must be clean for whatever change comes into your
life."

Mary didn't understand all that her mother said, but she du-
tifully steamed and scrubbed, and hoped she was as clean as she was
supposed to be. It was too dark in the lodge to see.

Little Bear Woman's place in the world was as set as the place
on the south side of the tent, next to the eastward opening door.
Here she had racks to hold her bowls and spoons, her fire tools, and
all the other things a woman needed for cooking; buckets of fresh
water with gourd dippers for drinking; her tanning tools; extra rawhide cases to hold sinew (used as thread) and beads and porcupine
quills; and her earth paints, for sometimes she painted her cases and
even Mary's moccasins.

Little Bear Woman's bed was just beyond her work area, and
beside it, on the floor, there was a pallet of worn old hides with
blankets piled on them, where Mary slept. A Cheyenne woman was
as sure of her place in the world as she was of her place in the dwell-
ing. Maheo, the Above Person, had said it should be so, and so it
was.

About the time of her first sweat bath, when she was feeling
very grown-up, Mary began to realize that her own place in the
Cheyenne world was not as secure as her mother's. They went to the
trading post one day. Mr. Abraham, behind the counter, looked at
Mary closely.

"She's pretty," he said in bad Cheyenne. "Getting to look like
her father, too."

"She is Cheyenne," Little Bear Woman answered stiffly.

"Only half," Mr. Abraham grinned. "Someday she'll have to
live like her father and learn white man's ways. You wait and see."

"What did he mean?" Mary asked, on the way home. She sat in
front of her mother, on the high-pommeled old-fashioned woman's
saddle, and she had to tip her head backward to speak clearly.

"He meant that someday you will have to go away to school
with other children," Little Bear Woman replied. "Someday you
will have to learn many things you can't learn here."

"Can't I go to the school at Darlington?" Mary asked. "I could stay at home, then, and live with you and Uncle."

"You would have to ford the river every day," her mother said. "Perhaps sometimes the water will be up, and you won't be able to get to the school, or come home. It would be better to live at the school, I think."

"When I go to school," Mary replied, "I will go far away, then. That way, I can't see you, or get so homesick."

"We'll see," was her mother's only answer.

It was that same summer that Mary really was aware for the first time of the Sun Dance, although later she could not recall it in exact detail. Like all the children, she knew there was a great bustle of preparation. Friends and relatives and visitors from other tribes came into camp, and there was a lot of cooking to do because everyone had to be fed. Mary's short legs trotted back and forth along the path to the riverbank so many times, as she carried buckets of water for stew and coffee, that they ached. Mary wished she were older. The older girls always went in twos, and shared the work of carrying buckets, but the little girls went alone, whenever their mothers sent them. Sometimes Mary thought her mother must use more water than any other woman in camp.

After the Cheyennes had gathered—everyone who could come, came—there were four quiet, serious days. A big tipi was put up east of the camp. It always looked sloppy and lopsided to the women, because this one time in the year the men put up a tipi, and they weren't very good at it. East of the tipi a tripod stood, with a medicine bundle hung from it. Mary asked her mother what the medicine was, but Little Bear Woman only said, "Be quiet. That belongs to the men. You aren't supposed to know about it."

There were four days of ceremonies in the Lone Tipi, as Mary's uncle called it. He went there with the other older men early in the morning and they prayed and fasted all day. Mary could hear them singing, but the tipi was too far away for her to make out the words. She only knew that these were serious songs, solemn songs, and that the name of Maheo, the Above Person, was repeated over and over again. Only the men and boys went near. All the women and girls had to stay away. Little Bear Woman said that was because Maheo's power was so great that he could hurt any woman who went too close.

On the fourth day all the women and girls stayed in their tents until sundown. Like the men, they fasted and prayed, but they also kept out of sight. Little Bear Woman said that was because on that day the bundle was opened, and the men and boys could see its contents. Any women who looked would lose her vision.

The women also kept very quiet. A Kiowa woman, who had come to visit and see the Sun Dance, sat in the tipi with them. Like Little Bear Woman, she kept her head bowed, and her lips moved ceaselessly, silently. They were praying, Mary knew. She had asked what they prayed for, and if she could pray, too, and her mother told her anyone could pray to Maheo for his blessing. So Mary prayed to Maheo, as well as she could, until her head nodded and she fell asleep in the quiet tent, leaning against her mother.

She awakened when the men returned. The long day was over, and the short summer dusk of the Plains was already turning to darkness. Her uncle and brothers sat quietly, waiting, while the women made broth and biscuits. Then everyone drank a little water—the first all day—and followed it with light food. Uncle prayed again, and they all went to sleep without talking.

The next morning was different: The four days of Sun Dance began! There was stir and bustle in the camp again. Men brought out their best horses, and painted them—not with power designs, but with pretty ones of open hands and animal heads. The women cooked a big breakfast, and then all the members of the family dressed in their best and combed their hair and painted the parting and their faces. This was the day to cut the holy center pole for the Sun Dance lodge.

In the middle of the circle of camps a second circle had been marked out by the priests, with an opening to the east. Now all the young men rode out of camp, past the Lone Tipi, down to the trees by the river. They rode joyously, as if they were going out to fight, and they sang their war songs. The older men followed them more slowly until the party reached the trees. Then the older men took the lead. One at a time, the men inspected the cottonwood trees in the grove, "until one was right."

The Sun Dance priest took his big double-bitted axe and signed to his wife to come forward. He cut the tree four times, one cut on each side, and then his wife finished chopping it down. She was careful to cut it so the leaves fell to the east and the butt end pointed toward the camp. The young men chopped off the branches down to the main fork, and then hitched ropes to the tree trunk. They also cut and stripped to the main fork thirty-six smaller trees. Women gathered up the branches and other brush, and, their arms filled with green, they mounted the horses behind the men. Everybody sang, loud gay songs.

"Why does Shell Woman ride with her brother-in-law?" Mary asked her mother.

"Because today they have the right," Little Bear Woman replied. "If her sister died, she could marry him, you know. Today they can flirt and laugh like young people, as if they were courting."

And it was to the music of courting songs that the whole party dragged the pole and carried the green branches back to camp, where the older men had already dug a deep hole to receive the tree trunk.

The pole lay on the ground, "like a man who had been hurt," pointing at the hole. With war songs and shouts the men attacked it. They painted four bands around the base of the pole, two red and two black; and then, all together, they raised it in its place and tamped the earth firmly down to hold it upright.

Now there were other poles to be put in place. Twelve were set upright, in holes in the ground, in a circle around the center pole. Twelve more were lashed from fork to fork of the circle of poles, to link them together. And then twelve poles were stretched from the crotches of the circle and lashed to the center pole, for rafters.

"Come," said Little Bear Woman. "The sun is high and everyone is hungry. Aren't you?"

"My stomach is making noises," said Mary.

"Then we should put something in it, and in the men's," remarked her mother.

Stew and sour-dough biscuits left from breakfast were heated while the coffeepot came to a boil. Little Bear Woman opened one of her rawhide cases and took out cakes of choke cherries pounded with honey and fat for dessert. It was a feast!

The Kiowa woman's husband, Little Bluff, came back with Mary's uncle and brothers. They were all hot and sweaty from the hard work they had been doing.

"I'm going to the river and swim," said Little Bluff.

"Let's all go," Uncle agreed, and the men left the camp. When they came back they looked fresh again, and Uncle was laughing.

"I think every man in camp had the same idea," he told them. "The river was full of them, like fish!"

"I want to go, too," Mary begged her mother.

"Later. After we eat and put things away, the women will go."

They sat down, some inside the tents and some just outside, and waited while Uncle asked Maheo to bless the food for them and to send them long life, happiness, and many friends. Then Little Bear Woman filled the enamelware bowls with stew and coffee, and gave them biscuits to use for spoons. Because there was company and this was a special feast, she even broke up a piece of the brown sugar the Mexicans brought when they came trading, to go in the coffee. When the meal was over, the men lighted their pipes and smoked and talked. The women rubbed the food bowls with clean sand, and when the tent was clean and tidy again, they went in their turn to the river to swim.

Swimming was not the same as bathing. When you bathed in the sweat lodge, it was a serious business, to get not only your body but your mind clean. If you spoke at all, it was to pray. But swimming in the river was fun. The women called to each other. The little girls pulled each other's hair, and some of the older ones dared to duck clear under the water. They pulled each other's feet, and kicked back, and laughed some more. It was all a change after the four solemn days when the men and boys were shut up in the Lone Tipi and nobody could make any noise.

Then Mary heard Uncle's voice calling, as if he were the camp crier. "Come, all you women!" he shouted.

"Come on," said Little Bear Woman. "It's time to go back."

Still laughing and chattering, the women and girls came out of the river. They took off the old clothes they had worn for swimming and put on fresh, clean ones they had left lying on the bank. All together, the women went back to camp.

Uncle was still calling. "Come here to the lodge, everybody," he repeated. "This is the time to make the special offering to

Maheo, the Above Person. Chases-His-Enemies will be here with the white buffalo hide in a moment."

Mary wondered where Chases-His-Enemies could have found a white buffalo. There were no buffaloes anymore, not even brown ones. When she turned with the others and looked to the east to see him coming, she understood. This buffalo had been killed a long time ago. The old men had saved it from one Sun Dance to the next.

Chases-His-Enemies rode four times around the lodge, so everyone could see the white buffalo hide. From the east, to the south, to the west, to the north he rode, and each time he was opposite the east doorway of the lodge, he stopped and called aloud.

"Look, you people," he cried. "Maheo has been good to us. He has given us a white buffalo, to remind us of the white buffalo woman who won the great race against the enemies of the Cheyennes, and gave us her body and those of her people for our food."

Mary had heard the myth of the white buffalo woman and the great race against the birds as long as she could remember. Both her mother and her uncle had told it to her as soon as she could understand anything serious. It was one of the sacred mysteries of Maheo, they said, and the Cheyennes must never forget it. She knew what the white buffalo hide stood for, and how important it was.

Chases-His-Enemies rode into the lodge and got down from his horse. Three times he tried to lift the white buffalo hide from the horse's back, and the fourth time he succeeded. He tried again, four times, to spread it at the foot of the center pole, and the fourth time he spread it on the ground.

It was Uncle's turn to come forward. In each hand he held a figure cut out of rawhide. One was shaped like a buffalo, and was black, to represent Mother Earth and her gifts to her children. The other was red and in human form, for it represented man and battles, and the power of the Sun Father.

"Come, all you people," Uncle summoned them. "Bring your offerings, and tie them to this hide."

Little Bear Woman gave Mary a piece of blue cloth, so pretty Mary wanted to keep it. But her mother pushed her gently forward, and when Mother tied a beaded blanket strip to the hide, Mary knotted on her piece of cloth.

"Now Maheo will surely bless you, because you gave him something you wanted for yourself," Little Bear Woman told her approvingly. Mary wondered why her mother knew she wanted the piece of cloth, but she did not ask.

With two forked sticks, Chases-His-Enemies raised the hide to the crotch of the center pole. When it was in place, Uncle raised a small tin food bucket, all shiny and new, and the two rawhide figures to the fork; they stayed there somehow, without being tied. "Maheo keeps them there," Mother whispered.

It was time to go back to camp. The men had to be fed before they went into the lodge that evening and began another four days' fast. Every man did not dance the Sun Dance—only those who wished to pray for special blessings for themselves or the members of their families. The men who did not take part ate and drank as little as possible during these four sacred days of the Sun Dance.

After supper, the men were very busy. They laid a thick bed of sage—the tall, fragrant, blue-gray man-sage—around the inside curve of the lodge, and over it they laid quilts the women brought from the camp. This was the place where the dancers would rest and smoke when they were not dancing.

Next the Sun Dance priest built the altar. He brought a blanket filled with white sand, spread it on the west side of the lodge, and covered it with sage. Four men brought him eight willow branches, two apiece, and he stripped their leaves from them and laid the leaves with the sage bed. Then he put the rods in the ground and bent them over to form four arches, like the curves of the rainbow.

Now the camp was still. Women and children clustered in front of their tents, but no one spoke. The priest went to his tent, and came out carrying his long red stone pipe, with the feathered stem. He had taken off all his clothes but his breech clout and moccasins, and his hair hung loose over his shoulders.

Behind the priest came his first wife, Shining Woman. She was old, and was greatly respected because she had been a sacred woman and would now teach the new sacred woman. Like her husband, she was stripped to the waist, with a blanket belted around her. She was barefoot, and her hair swung on her shoulders, partly hiding her dangling old woman's breasts. In her hands she grasped a buffalo skull, holding it by the horns. The mouth and nostril openings were stuffed with sweet grass; one side was painted red and the other black. Bending forward with the weight of the skull, Shining

Woman walked behind her husband, and entered the lodge after him.

Behind them came the dancers and their sponsors, for each man had an older one who would tell him what to do, pray with him, and paint him for the four days. They followed the priest and Shining Woman into the lodge, and all filed around the inside four times. Then at last they took their places, the priest and his wife behind the buffalo skull and rainbow-shaped altar, for Shining Woman had placed the skull in front of the willow arches, facing outward, toward the people. Mary, her mother, and the rest of the women sat outside the lodge frame and watched.

Each dancer sat in the same place his sponsor had once occupied, and his sponsor sat beside him. The drummers brought a rolled-up piece of buffalo rawhide and special drumsticks made of new bois d'arc wood; the heads were made of bull scrotums and held pebbles, so they were drumsticks and rattles at the same time. The head drummer struck the hide with his stick, and the singing began.

One at a time, as their sponsors directed them, the dancers rose and stood facing the center pole, their eyes fixed on the bright tin bucket, which shone in the light of a little fire between the pole and the altar. With eagle wing–bone whistles in their mouths, the dancers flexed their legs and danced in place. The sound of the whistles, and of the drumming and singing, seemed to Mary to fill the world—to be all of the sounds in the world.

Now the priest rose at the end of the fourth song, and all the sounds stopped together.

"Listen to me, all you people," the priest began. "This is our sacred time of the year. This is the time when we sacrifice all we have to Maheo: our possessions, our bodies, our hunger and thirst and pain. Whatever we do, we must do just right; there must be no mistakes in anything.

"If one of the dancers gets too tired to go on, he must stop and rest a little before he spoils the dance. His sponsor will tell him what to do if that happens. Remember, all you young men. You do not pledge to dance one Sun Dance only. You must dance four times, once a year for four years, before all your prayers can be answered. If you do not carry out this vow, something bad will happen to you.

"Children! You must be quiet and respectful while this dance is going on. Don't run around the camp and laugh and shout. Stay with your mothers, and do what they tell you. Be good in every way you know.

"Women! You are not forgotten or left out of this dance. My wife is here for you. And Sand, who is chief pledger of the dance, has his wife with him too. They can come in now."

Very slowly Sand and his wife, Willow, who would be the new sacred woman, came into the lodge and circled it four times. They were middle-aged, not old. After the fourth round, Willow sat down beside Shining Woman, the priest's wife, who had been a sacred woman in an earlier Sun Dance. There the two women would remain, fasting and not drinking, until the end of the dance, except when the priest excused them to go out for a few minutes.

The second set of dance songs began. These seemed like the sounds of water, and their coolness brought the coolness of the night to wrap around Mary. She huddled close to her mother, and dozed. Little Bear Woman and some of the others were singing with the men, and Mary could feel her mother's body vibrate with the song. When she waked, Mary tried to learn the songs and hum with the other women. They sat there until the midnight star was over-head and the dancers lay down to rest.

"Do you have the Sun Dance, too?" Mary asked the Kiowa woman in the morning. They were scrubbing the bowls, and making the tent tidy, while Little Bear Woman cooked fried bread and coffee and stew.

"We used to have it," the visitor answered. Tears came into her eyes. "Our young men lost interest after they went away to school. When they came back, the man who guarded the *Taime*—our sacred figure, like your rawhide ones—had died, and there was no one to carry it on. So we lost it."

"Will that happen to the Cheyennes?" Mary asked.

"Perhaps. Who knows? Many things are changing now. Once a camp like this would have been all tipis, without any tents. Now there are many tents, and people even live in houses." She wiped the tears away. "Some of the new things are good, like cooking stoves and bowls that don't break or wear out. But some of us still miss the old days and the old ways. So when we hear that the Cheyennes or the Arapahoes—or even the Sioux, away to the north—are having a

Sun Dance we try to go, so we can remember and feel young again."

It was a strange thought to Mary—to want to feel young again. Why, she could hardly wait to be grown-up, and here was this grown woman crying to be a little girl. Mary couldn't understand it.

It was midmorning before Little Bear Woman finished cooking. She gave Mary the clothes basket full of fried bread to carry, and she and their friend hung the kettles of stew and coffee on a pole and carried it between them to the lodge.

All over the camp women were streaming from their tents to the lodge, all carrying food.

"Why do we do this?" Mary asked.

"Because they are going to change the paints," answered Little Bear Woman, as if that explained everything.

Inside the lodge there was a lot going on. The dancers and their sponsors stood over buckets of water, sponging the paint from their bodies with bunches of sage. The Sun Dance priest was already putting fresh paint on Sand, the man who was the chief pledger. The two women had left the lodge. When they returned, the other women clustered about them while they washed and repainted each other. Finally, the sponsors dipped twigs of the yellow-gray woman-sage in water and drew them between the dancers' lips. This was the only liquid the dancers might have.

Now everyone sat quietly on the sage bed, and the women from the camp began to carry in their containers of food. Each one set the food before one of the dancers. Little Bear Woman pointed with her lips to Mary's youngest brother, and Mary set the basket of fried bread before him. She wondered as she did it why no one had told her he was going to dance. She hardly recognized him now, with his face and body painted and his eyes looking somewhere else—perhaps inside himself, at the things in his heart.

Each dancer spoke through his sponsor, and each sponsor called the name of a friend or visitor who was to receive the food. This was to prove that the dancers didn't have to eat; they were strong enough to look at food and give it away and give other people their blessings. Shell Woman's son called Mary's name, although the fact that his mother had named her made her almost his sister. Mary slipped into the lodge and stood before him. He gestured to a bowl of fruit his sister had placed on the ground, and Mary picked it up. It was a big bowl, full of fruits from the trading post. She knew the names of some of them: apples, oranges, and pears. But there were some long skinny yellow things she had never seen before. She didn't know what they were.

When the gifts had been distributed and the men's bodies had been repainted, the families went back to their camps. There were many visitors to be fed, including the Agent and the teachers.

One teacher, who was really the head man of the school, was Mary's favorite. His name was Johnny Seger, but the Indians called him Johnny Schmoker because he always sang a song he had learned when he was a little boy at home. The Indians did not know German, but they liked the sound of the words even though they had no meaning for them.

> Johnny Schmoker, Johnny Schmoker,
> Ich kann spiel on,
> Ich kann spiel on
> Meine kleine tootlesack.
> Rach, rach, rach,
> Dis ist meine tootlesack.

He always had a big black cigar in his mouth and smoke trailing behind him like the locomotives on the trains that came into Fort Reno.

After Johnny Seger and the other visitors left, Mary was very busy helping her mother clean the dishes and put the food near the fire so it would be warm if other visitors should come.

The next day there were many more Indians visiting the camp, but no white people. Those who came the day before had seen the dance, satisfied their curiosity, and feasted, so they stayed away.

This morning, when Little Bear Woman and Mary took food to the lodge, her mother said, "What you will see after the paints are changed is very sacred and very secret. You must never speak about it except to another Cheyenne."

Nothing in the lodge seemed to have changed when they got there. The men were resting or bathing; the two women had gone out to the latrine area, and everyone seemed quiet and peaceful. But this time the men had not yet been painted. No one carried food into the lodge until the men gathered and were all painted. Then the women put the buckets and bowls on the floor as before, and the gifts were distributed.

Now there was a sudden change of feeling. Old men came into the lodge and stood behind the sponsors, for they had themselves sponsored those men. Each one carried a braided rawhide rope, and each handed the rope and some small sticks to his own pupil.

"What are they going to do?" Mary whispered.

"The young men will make the sacrifice of themselves," her mother murmured in reply.

While everyone watched, the young men stood up, their whistles already in their mouths. The sponsors stood behind the dancers as before. But each of the older men held a sharp stone knife in his right hand now, and with the knife he pierced the skin of the young man's chest, making two holes on each side. Then the sponsor thrust a pointed stick through each set of holes, tied a small rope to either end of each stick, and finally, with a longer, heavier rope, linked the loops on the sticks to the center pole of the lodge.

The drumming and singing began again, the dancers' whistles took up their monotonous sound, and the men danced in place as they had before. This time the dancers leaned backward, throwing their whole weight against the ropes and the sticks. Blood ran down their chests and stained the ground. Their feet churned the earth, until each man danced in a pool of bloody mud.

Mary felt sick as she watched them; watched her relatives and their friends pull with all their strength against the bindings that held them to the pole. Some of the men began to weaken; some were too tired to blow their whistles. Others would stop dancing for a time, and then start dancing when they had rested. But the sound of the whistles went on and on, the beating of the feet went on and on until one young man gave a great cry and fell to the ground. The sticks had pulled free from his skin, and two great raw strips of flesh hung down his chest, with the muscles showing white where he had jerked free. Mary hid her face in her hands. She could not stand to look.

"Sit up," her mother scolded under her breath. "You are a Cheyenne. This dance is called Standing Against the Enemy, and unless you can face an enemy you may be killed someday yourself. Watch how brave your men are."

The two women behind the altar were weeping softly, but no one else shed any tears.

"Why are they crying?" Mary asked.

"Because tonight the younger one must make her great sacrifice," Little Bear Woman replied. "She, too, must give her body, but to the other woman's husband, and in the dark. Then they will know the dance is complete, and power has passed from one man to the other."

There was something in her mother's voice that forbade more questions. Something hushed, as if she were afraid to speak the words, even to her own child.

"Someday you will understand," she added, still in that hushed voice.

The paints were changed again in midafternoon, and they all went home to rest. Their Kiowa friends had gone to visit in another camp, and Little Bear Woman held Mary close as they slept on a pile of old army blankets.

In the evening, the two of them drank some soup and ate cold fried bread alone. All the men were at the lodge, the visitors were away, and their tent was peaceful. It was what Johnny Schmoker called "homelike." That was almost the only English word that Mary knew, and she wasn't sure what it meant, but she knew it must be a good meaning from the tone in which he said it. She was almost sorry when Little Bear Woman said, "It is time to go back to the lodge."

Inside the lodge everything was quiet, too. The men who were not taking part in the dance were building a little hut, like a sweat lodge, away beside the Lone Tipi. They were quiet, too, giving their directions to each other almost in whispers.

When the little lodge was finished the men returned to the dance lodge and sat on the ground around it, behind the dancers. There was a long time of waiting, people sitting with their heads bowed and their lips moving in silent prayer, and then the Sun Dance priest stood up and spoke.

"Now we have come to the most holy time of the dance," he began. "The time when women must prove that their bravery is equal to men's. This woman has come here with her husband, to take a share of the Sun Dance power from me and give it to him. All of you sit quietly and wait until we know that she has succeeded."

Willow and Shining Woman rose, and followed the priest out to the lodge by the Lone Tipi, and Shining Woman lifted the blanket curtain that covered its door. Then she stood aside while her husband and the other woman went in.

The priest's wife stood there, guarding the door, for what seemed to Mary like a very long time. Something about it all frightened Mary, even though she didn't know just what was happening. Perhaps it was the stillness, and the feeling that something would be changed for all these people when the ceremony was over.

The biggest star was directly overhead, and its six smaller brothers had turned to the north, when the priest's wife raised the door curtain and the others emerged. In her left hand, Willow held a white eagle feather. That was surprising: Cheyenne women were never supposed to handle eagle feathers. It would change the color of their skin, giving it white patches all over.

Very slowly, the priest leading, the two women returned to the Sun Dance lodge. They stopped three times on the way, before they entered. When the priest and his wife had taken their places, Willow handed the feather to her husband.

"I have succeeded," she said. Then all four went back to the little lodge, but only the pledger and his wife entered it. The Sun Dance priest and his wife stood outside, like guards. At last the pledger and his wife came out. This time the man had the feather, tied to his scalp lock.

The fourth day was the end of the dance. The dancers and their sponsors were very tired now. The old men dipped the sage sprigs deeper into the water and drew them more slowly through the younger men's lips. Two dancers lay back on the sage bed, while their sponsors fanned them with eagle wings.

"Are they sick?" Mary asked her mother.

"They have gone away for now," Little Bear Woman said slowly. "Perhaps they are having visions."

"When they wake up, will they tell what they saw?"

"Perhaps. Some men lose power if they tell their visions; for others it is strengthened by telling and sharing. When they wake up, we may know."

The gifts were brought and the paints changed for the last time when the sun stood directly overhead. This time there were many gifts besides food: people brought blankets and shawls and painted hides. They brought new kettles and bowls, filled to the brim with food and coffee. All these presents went to visitors from other tribes, or to old Cheyennes who needed them.

Why didn't they give presents to children, too? Mary wondered. Children liked to be given presents as much as anybody. But the giving went on, always to old people or to strangers, until the afternoon shadows began to lengthen.

It was time for the last dance. The priest rose, and all the young men stood up with him. The drumming and singing also rose, stronger and harder than ever. The blasts of the whistles cut through Mary's head, so that she wondered how the dancers could stand the sound. The force of their power—all of them: sacred women, dancers, singers—became a great wind that swept across the prairie and caught up the watching people. Everyone was singing, with the women's voices rising above the men's in a great worshipping chorus. Only the young man who had fallen in the dance when the sticks pulled loose from his chest lay on his bed of sage.

The priest rapped with an eagle-wing fan on the wilted-willow rainbow arches before him. He turned, where he stood on the east side of the lodge, and all the young men dropped their whistles from their mouths and turned as he did, to the east.

First one, then another, then all the dancers ran through the side of the lodge. The priest followed, driving them forward with his fan. They ran to the south and to the west, and then, the last time, to the north. From there they ran to their camps. The priest trampled down the willow altars, and the new sacred woman carried the sacred buffalo skull out. The drummers threw their drumsticks down on what was left of the rawhide slab drum, and everyone who could get into the lodge rushed forward to seize one. Mary was little and quick, and she got there first. She clutched the drumstick tightly in one hand, her present from the Sun Dance.

"It is a great blessing," Little Bear Woman said, when Mary returned to her. "Always keep it and you will always be well."

"Oh," said the child. "I thought it was a present."

"A very great present," her mother assured her.

3

SCHOOL DAYS

Summers and Sun Dances came and went. There was always the same excitement of anticipation, always the bustle of cooking, always the piercing sound of the whistles. The children ran about the camps, fluttering like little swallows, and taking it all as a matter of course.

The fall that Mary was twelve, when the excitement was over and the visitors had gone, Little Bear Woman said to her, "It's time for you to go to school."

"What school?" Mary asked apprehensively. She had heard older girls and boys talk about a school in Carlisle, Pennsylvania—a strange, faraway place with a strange name.

"This school here, at Darlington. It was built for the Arapahoes but it takes Cheyennes now."

"Oh," Mary said, relieved. "Then I can stay at home, and not have to go away."

"You can stay at the school, and come home on Saturdays, because you can't cross the river every day. But the rest of the time you should stay there and learn what a white woman does."

"Why?" Mary asked. "I know what a Cheyenne woman does now."

"You are half a white woman," Little Bear Woman said, sadly. "You must learn their ways."

She was the only person who had never reminded Mary that her father was white. By this time, Mary was used to having the other children call her White Girl and tease her about her gray-blue eyes. She was used to being left out of certain games, and being told they were only for Cheyennes. She was used to going home and practicing games alone, and she knew she could play them as well as anybody. She was used to the whole business, and didn't let it worry her too much. Only her mother had seemed to forget it. And now she was making a point of it!

To school Mary went. Her mother took her hand on the day the school bell rang for the first time, and they walked to Darlington School, wading across the river when they came to it. Mary's extra clothes and her porcupine-tail hairbrush were tied in a bundle in an extra shawl. She had new moccasins on her feet, and a pair of silver earrings swung from her ears. She knew she looked as nice as any girl in camp.

Johnny Schmoker (Seger) was still the principal, and they went to see him first. He smiled around his cigar and asked, "Did she want to come?" One of the older students interpreted for him.

"She should come," Little Bear Woman told him. "She must learn white people's ways, so she can live in their world."

"She's very small," Johnny Schmoker observed doubtfully.

"She is twelve," said Little Bear Woman. "That is time for her to begin to learn."

"Suppose she runs away and goes home? Many students do."

"Then I will bring her back. But she won't run away. Will you?" she asked, looking at her daughter.

"No." Mary hung her head. That very minute she had been thinking how to do it; how to get away from this place and home to camp.

"Because if you do," her mother said fiercely, "I will beat you before I bring you back. Remember that."

"I will remember. I promise not to run away."

"Then she is yours," Little Bear Woman said to Johnny Schmoker, and put Mary's hand in his. She turned and walked out of the building.

"Not like any other Cheyenne woman I ever saw," Johnny Schmoker said to the interpreter. "Usually they fight like cats to keep their kittens."

The interpreter repeated his words in Cheyenne, and Mary knew her mother had surprised Johnny.

It was at Darlington School that she got the name of Mary.

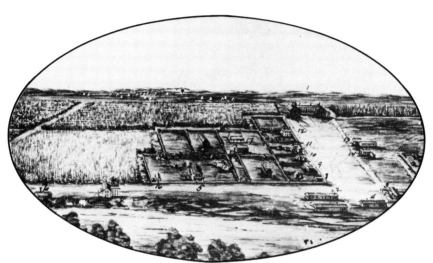

Drawing of the Cheyenne-Arapaho Agency, 1878.

The Mission at Darlington.

John H. Seger, the Principal of Mary's first school.

The original school building at Seger Colony.

Indian girls at Seger's school.

Schoolboys cleaning up the grounds of the Seger Indian School.

Johnny Seger called all the boys John or Joe and all the girls Mary or Minnie or Martha, with their mothers' Indian names added on, so he could tell them apart.

There was lots to do besides go to school at Darlington.

Mornings began when they all marched into the dining hall to the strains of "America, America," which one of the teachers played on the piano. Then Johnny himself said the blessing, and they all sat down with a loud scraping of chairs. At every place there was a large glass of milk, from the cows on the school farm. They could drink it right down or pour it on their oatmeal, but one way or another, every child had to swallow that glass of milk before he got any pancakes or hot biscuits or anything else.

After breakfast they all marched to their quarters, where they were given fifteen minutes to make the beds that had been airing, hang up their clothes, and put everything in order. "Just as if the Government inspector were coming," Johnny Schmoker always said.

Winter and summer the boys took the donkey and cart and policed the grounds, while the girls cleaned up the kitchen and got everything ready for dinner. Then they were ready for classes, which lasted until an hour before noon dinner, when they were all dismissed. The students who had details in the kitchen or dining room went to work, but everyone else, no matter what the weather was like, went outside for "physical exercise." Sometimes the students drilled in military formation with broom handles for guns. Sometimes they did calisthenics. And once a month, when the music teacher came, the students had folk dancing. Mary liked that best of all. The big boys moved the piano out on the porch and the music teacher sat facing the students and conducted.

"ONE and two and THREE and four . . . ," she would count, and the students would follow the beat, pointing their toes and trying to catch the strange rhythm that went UP and down instead of DOWN and up.

After everybody was warmed up and hungry from the "physical exercises," they all went into the dining hall for dinner.

This time one of the older boys, in rotation, would ask the blessing, bowing his head so that nobody could make out what he said.

"You must be a great friend of the Father Above," was a standard after-dinner joke. "You talk so nobody else can hear you."

After dinner, the students all worked. The girls sewed and did domestic chores, while the boys worked in the garden, cut wood, and fenced in cattle. Johnny Seger had been a farmer before he was as old as most of these boys, and he was determined to make farmers of them if it was humanly possible. Sometimes it seemed that it wasn't. He gave them a long talk one day about organic fertilizers, and the next day he came out and found that the Cheyenne boys had emptied the cesspools and spread the contents on his newly plowed vegetable beds.

After Mary had been at school for what seemed to her like a long time, Johnny Seger called the students together in the dining hall after breakfast. Mary and her friend Martha did not yet speak English well and they thought he said: "Listen to me. I have talked to the Agent, and he has asked me to open a school and farming colony. It will be sixty miles away from Darlington, and will be for the families of my former students, who are mostly Arapahoes. It will take a while to get the buildings ready so the people can move in. We will stay on here—everybody but the work crews—until they are finished. Then we will go to the new colony."

"That isn't fair," Mary said to Martha afterward. "Just the Arapahoes. There are plenty of Cheyennes who can work, too."

"Maybe," said Martha. "He spoke in English and we don't understand too well." They were swinging on the wild grapevines that looped tree to tree beside the river. "Maybe Cheyennes just don't want to work."

"I don't know if we understood him. But I want to go to his school. When I can understand English better I'll ask him if he will take Cheyennes. I want to be a teacher when I grow up. I'll make a lot of money. No one is going to call me a lazy Cheyenne."

One summer Mary's mother took her home. Mary did not understand why but she enjoyed being back in camp.

It was a long, hot, dry, dusty summer. The go-devils twisted across the flats at noontime, and then there was no more wind until late late evening, when it rustled through the leaves of the cottonwoods as if it were blowing them flat.

One morning Mary's mother called her into the tent. "We will have to start getting ready for next year's Sun Dance," she told her daughter. "We have no part in this year's, but next year Uncle will put up the lodge."

Mary began to realize that next year's Sun Dance would be different from the others she had watched. Little Bear Woman kept her busy. The men killed as many steers as they could trade for, and Mary was put to work scraping the meat off the inner sides of the hides. It was hot, smelly, dirty work, but when she complained, her mother told her to be thankful for a dry summer, and went on with her own, harder work, which was peeling the hair off the outer surfaces of the hides Mary had fleshed. Every few days they added another clean rawhide to the stack that was growing in the back of the tent.

When all the hides they could get had been fleshed and scraped, the really heavy work began. For this, Little Bear Woman sent for her woman cousins, from the Sewing Women's Society, since Mary was not yet strong enough to pull and work her part of the hide.

They cooked a mixture of brains, liver, and tallow and mixed it into a paste. The organs had been drying ever since the animals were killed.

"Every hide should have brains enough to tan itself," said Shell Woman, laughing. She was too old to handle a full hide herself anymore, but she could watch and supervise the other women. There were some small calfskins in the pile, and Shell Woman and Mary worked on those.

They rubbed the brains-liver-tallow compound into the grain of the hide with flat, round stones. Every woman had her own stones, which she carefully put away after using them. Before they did anything else, Shell Woman had taken Mary out to the riverbank, and they had walked along it, looking carefully for the right kind of stones—ones that were round, with curved surfaces to fit the palm of a woman's hand, and without sharp edges.

"You must get your stones first," Shell Woman had said. "The other tools will come later, if you are a good worker."

Once, when reaching for a stone, Shell Woman's sleeve had slipped up her arm, revealing a double row of little blue tattoo marks that stretched from the old lady's wrist to the bend of her elbow.

"What are those for?" Mary had asked.

Shell Woman had slid her sleeve down again. "Those are the hides that I have tanned," she said. "In the old days, every woman kept a record like that."

"I thought they kept them on their scraper handles."

"Not when I was young," Shell Woman had replied. Her eyes went far back, searching the past. "In the old days, when we were fighting, fighting all the time, we could lose our tools. I suppose we could have lost our arms, too," she said, and smiled. "We didn't think about that. We kept our records with us always."

They went on gathering stones until they had four that were the right size and shape. Some were thinner than others, and two had small rounded points jutting out, so they could be fitted into the curves of the hide. Just river pebbles, but Mary thought they were beautiful.

A lot of things happened that summer. Mary herself became a woman. At first she was frightened at the flow of blood, but her mother and Shell Woman reassured her. It was natural and right, they said, but she must stay away from men and the things men used while it was going on. So she spent four dull days a month in a little brush arbor her mother built to shelter her, and only her friend Martha could come and talk to her. Even Shell Woman stayed away, because she was busy directing the other women's work on the hides. If they could have done with less direction, they were all too polite to say so.

At the end of each of her periods, Little Bear Woman made Mary take a sweat bath, and then dip in the river, so she would be clean. Mary was old enough to be married now, her mother told her, but when Mary said she would rather go on to school, no one insisted on marriage. Perhaps a time had come when it was important for a girl to know as much, and the same things, as a boy.

But in between the times she spent in the little arbor, Mary worked on the calfskins with Shell Woman. The old lady showed her the right movement, rolling from the shoulder, with the full weight of her body behind it, to press and work the brains and liver into the skin, first on one surface and then on the other. Then they sprinkled the hides with warm water, and rolled them up "to rest," as Shell Woman said, overnight.

In the morning, Mary and Shell Woman sat on the ground, facing each other, with the hide between them. Working forward and back, to and away from each other, they pulled and stretched each skin until it was as soft and supple as cloth. This was the real tanning; everything they had done before had been accomplished to work up to this point. As each hide was finished, it was sprinkled with dried wild sage, rolled up, and laid aside, while the work began on the next one. There were four calfskins, and at the end of the summer Shell Woman put four new, tiny tattoos on the inside of her forearm.

"Mark me, too," Mary said, holding out her hand.

"It will hurt," Shell Woman cautioned her.

"I worked hard for it," Mary insisted. "I want people to know what I can do."

"You talk like a Cheyenne," Shell Woman said, laughing. She pricked Mary's forearm and rubbed charcoal into the holes all the same. Mary was proud of her tattoo marks. They made her more Cheyenne than the other girls, she thought.

That was the summer, too, when the men made an expedition to the pipestone quarry in Minnesota. There were other stones that could be used for making pipes, but the soft red stone that cuts easily was the kind they needed to make ceremonial pipes.

Uncle and some of the other men missed the Sun Dance this year so they could get a good start on their trip. Mary watched her uncle and brothers get ready: each with a spare horse to carry back a pack of stone; each with his weapons, although they were not likely to meet any enemies; and each with eight pairs of moccasins, so they would have shoes on their feet at all times. It was like a war party getting ready to go, Little Bear Woman said. The men even took dried meat and mesquite meal with them, although they would meet friends on their travels and would be fed.

No woman might go on this trip, or see or touch the stone after it was brought back, until it had been ceremonially cleaned and made ready for working.

The waiting time was long and dull. Mary had not realized before how much space the men filled in the mother tent. Now they were gone, the place seemed very empty.

The big storm came during this time, too. All day long the sky had blazed like the inside of a polished brass kettle, but there was no sun. Late in the afternoon everything began to darken as if it had been rubbed with soot. It was not that the light went away, but that the darkness replaced it. The sky grew blacker and blacker, until one expected to see the stars, but there were no stars to be seen.

Then the wind began, first running along the earth like a frightened rabbit and then moving upward into the trees.

"The cottonwoods are talking to us," Mary cried. "Listen, Mother. They are trying to tell us something."

"They are trying to tell us to take shelter!" Little Bear Woman exclaimed. She seized Mary's hand, and they ran together to Shell Woman's tipi, where other women and children were clustered.

Why the tipi? Mary wondered, but after the storm passed, she knew why. The tents lay flat in the mud, their contents smashed and broken, all hit from the same angle—the southwest. But the few tipis stood proud and straight, their curves the best defense against the wind. None of them were hurt.

Long after true dark, Johnny Seger and the work party who were building houses for Arapaho families came in.

"Gone. All gone," Johnny said before anyone could ask him. "We built out on the flat. I thought we would be safe. But the wind took all our work—everything."

"You'd think even an Arapaho would know better than that!" Little Bear Woman said, disgusted. She shook her finger at Mary. "Remember this. Never build out on the flat; build in a grove of trees, where you will have some shelter."

"But the trees could blow down," Mary protested.

"They may, that's true. But trees are round, like tipis, and the wind will go around and between them before it knocks them down."

Mary never forgot. Years later, when she had houses of her own, she always made sure that they were set among the trees, for safety.

The Arapaho families were to have moved to Johnny's new houses that fall, but now they could not. Instead, everyone stayed on at Darlington Agency, and they were still there when the men came back with their loads of pipestone.

"We sent you a word when we got there," Uncle said when they were eating that night.

"You sent us a storm!" Little Bear Woman snapped. "We didn't need it! All the tents blown down, all the hides spoiled so we have had to do them all over again. . . ." She began to cry, and Mary, suddenly realizing for the first time how much work they had lost, cried with her.

"It broke the heat," Uncle said, as if he wanted to calm them down.

"Never mind the heat," Little Bear Woman replied. "We're all used to heat—in the summer, that is. Next time send a little rain, not a tornado."

"All right," said Uncle, and went on eating his supper. It seemed to Mary that he wanted them all to be peaceful and quiet— even more so than usual.

Every good day from then on, they continued to rework the hides. In time they were soft and smooth again, but every skin had a pink tinge from the mud where it had lain after the storm.

"Never give up," said Shell Woman. "Keep trying." Mary remembered the words and the way the old lady spoke them for the rest of her life.

And this also was the summer Martha changed her name. "I'm tired of all these Marys and Marthas," she announced defiantly. "If Sun Dance is the time for naming babies, it ought to be a time for changing to grown-up names, too."

"What name are you going to pick?" Mary asked in awe. Such a thing would never have occurred to her. Somebody gave you a name and that was it, unless someone else changed it.

"Minnie," said her girl friend. "I'm going to do it right, too, and have a give-away."

So in addition to working on Little Bear Woman's hides, Mary helped Martha get ready for her give-away. Shell Woman told them what to do, and showed them how.

"You must have four presents," she said, "one each for four people. And you must do it all yourselves, and give the presents to older people. What name have you chosen?" she asked Martha as Mary had.

"Minnie," Martha replied, and she pushed out her lower lip to show that she had made up her mind.

The two girls went to the trading post, and Mr. Abraham, because he liked the girls, gave them a present of a length of canvas and some red and yellow paint. The girls measured the fabric, and decided they had enough for two pairs of painted pillowcases. But that would be only two presents, and they needed two more. Mary solved the problem one day when they went for water.

"Why don't we make two backrests?" she asked, looking at a dogwood tree and its straight, smooth branches.

"Let's!" said Martha and they went to work, trimming off the branches from the dogwood tree as far up as they could reach. Little Bear Woman gave them sinew to tie the branches together.

"First you must peel them and scrape them clean," she reminded the two girls, and they spent many hours working with sharp stones until the wood was white and clean, and the branches equal in size. Shell Woman took no part in this. Her skill was with skins and cloth, not wood.

When the first day of the Sun Dance came, and the people were gathered in front of the Sun Dance lodge, the crier called the girls forward.

"Now we are going to see something new," he told the people. "A young woman is going to change her own name—not her Cheyenne name, but her school one. I never heard of this happening before. But times change, and people must change with them, I suppose." He turned to Martha. "Tell the people your new name, and call the ones who are to get your gifts," he instructed her.

"My new name is Minnie," Martha said. "I choose it for Mrs. Browning, because she is the nicest white lady I know. And I call her first to get her gift, because I have chosen her name."

Mrs. Browning came forward and took a pillowcase Minnie stretched out to her.

"Hah-hoh," she said. The first thing she had done when she came to Darlington was to learn the polite words in Cheyenne and Arapaho. So now she could say "Thank you" like a good Cheyenne woman.

"My next present"—another pillowcase—"goes to Shell Woman, who has helped my friend and me," Minnie said, and the crier repeated her words.

"This next present," Minnie said, holding up a backrest, "I

want to go to Little Bear Woman, the mother of my friend, Mary. She helped us, too.

"And this last present"—another backrest—"is for Sand's wife, because this is the fourth year they have put up a Sun Dance for us, and we are all grateful. Now I am Minnie. Pivé!"

It was the first time any Cheyenne girl had changed her own name. Mary wondered if it would be the last. And she thought Minnie was pretty silly about it, giving presents to people and acting like a young man who changed his name after his first battle. Nobody else said anything, but Mary wondered what they were thinking. Late that evening, she asked her mother what people said about Minnie.

"Nobody said anything," Little Bear Woman informed her. "Why should they? What was there to say?"

"Did they think it was a good thing to do?" Mary persisted.

"They just didn't say."

"But she went against the rules. If you do that, something bad will happen someday."

"Go to sleep," was all Little Bear Woman said, and before she could argue, Mary found she was asleep.

On the eventful night of that Sun Dance Mary found out two things. She was sitting on the fringes of the crowd of women when she felt someone put an arm around her from behind. At first she thought it was Minnie, playing a joke, and she pushed at the arm, and whispered, "Go away."

"I will if you come with me," a young man's voice answered.

"I won't. What do you want with me?"

"Just some fun, White Girl."

"What kind of fun?"

"Oh, you know. I want to take you, the way that man is taking the woman in the lodge. You know what men and women do when they lie down together. You're old enough."

Vaguely, Mary knew what he meant. Her mother had told her some things when she became a woman. But this was different from being with a man she was married to. This was wrong, somehow. She sprang to her feet, and pulled away from the man she could not see in the darkness. Crying, she searched for her mother.

"What is it? What is the trouble?" Little Bear Woman asked.

"A man. He took hold of me. He wanted—"

"I know what he wanted," Little Bear Woman snapped. "Who was he? Do you know? Did you go with him?"

"I don't know him," Mary sobbed. "I got away. I came to you. . . ."

"Be quiet," her mother soothed her. "If you came to me, you were right. You are safe here."

"I should have remembered that you are a woman now," Little Bear Woman said. "I should have sewn you into a blanket, under your dress, so no man could reach you."

"Would that be better?" Mary asked.

"It would protect you," her mother reassured her. "From now on, whenever we are going to be with a lot of people, I will do it. My own mother always did. And if you ever have a daughter, make sure she is protected that way, too. Cheyenne women are proud of being pure, and that is one thing they do that no other tribe does."

Another thought than her own danger took over Mary's mind. "Mother, the man said—in the little lodge Sand's wife and the priest were doing the same thing. . . ."

"That is different," Little Bear Woman said sternly. "What they are doing is sacred; it is very holy. That woman is making her sacrifice so that her husband will have greater power. Later they will share it with someone else, in the same way, because Sand will become a priest if she succeeds in winning the power."

Dimly, in the moonlight, Mary saw the door of the lodge open and two figures step out. Almost like ghosts they moved, the priest's wife behind them, back to the Sun Dance lodge. Sand's wife handed her husband the white eagle feather she carried. "I have succeeded," she murmured.

A little ripple of sound went around the lodge, as Sand and his wife, followed by the priest and his wife, left it for the little shelter.

"This is the heart of the Sun Dance," Little Bear Woman said. "This is the most sacred part. If a woman is willing to give her own body to strengthen her husband's power, she is very holy indeed."

"What if she has no husband?" Mary asked.

"She may serve her brother or her son in the same way," Little

Bear Woman assured her. "Then she is indeed Mah-hee-yuna, for she has given everything she can for her people."

The next day Mary and Minnie talked it over.

"I couldn't do that—not for anybody," Minnie said firmly.

"Not with my own brother," Mary added. "That's wrong. You must respect your brothers and not even look at them or speak to them, unless you need to."

"That's what my mother told me," Minnie agreed.

Later, Minnie's mother called both girls into her tent, and explained to them exactly what the relations between a man and a woman should be. "This can bring you both great joy or great shame," she finished. "That will depend on you and your man. What is done in secret and in hiding is bad. What is done with the knowledge and the blessing of the people is good. Remember that."

But it was of the shame that Mary found herself thinking afterward. More and more she wondered why, if the acts that went on in the little lodge had the blessing of the people and were good, they took place at night and in darkness. She wondered about it, but she did not like to ask questions; they must be unspoken. Mary began to have an uneasy feeling that to ask too many questions would bring out things about herself she did not want to know.

The long, eventful summer ended at last. Johnny took two teachers from Darlington and left for what was called "Seger Colony" with some Arapaho families.

"You can come if you want to," he told Mary as the wagons were being loaded.

"I thought you said just Arapahos. No Cheyennes," she reminded him.

"You're a little bit different," he said, and put his hand on her head, like a blessing.

But Mary stayed at Darlington, and went home on weekends, as she had the year before. She spoke English more fluently now, but some sounds she found hard to master. *Doctor* always came out of her mouth *noctor,* and *l* sounds turned into *n*'s. *R*'s she just passed over, slurring them into *eh*'s. Some of the other Cheyenne children spoke English well, and her poor speech bothered Mary so much that at last she spoke to her mother about it.

"It's because they come from a different band from ours," Little Bear Woman informed her. "All Cheyenne bands speak a little differently."

"Will I ever speak better?" Mary asked.

Her mother replied, "Just go on talking. People will understand you."

There were so many things to puzzle and worry about when you were growing up! How you spoke, and why you were different from the other Cheyenne girls; men and women and how they fitted together—all sorts of things.

Another puzzle was the heap of hides in the back of her mother's tent. It seemed to Mary that every time she came home from school on Saturday, her mother was working with the hides.

Some she beaded with horizontal stripes of red and yellow, divided into parts by two rows of black beads, and with red yarn tufts attached to them. When Little Bear Woman worked on these hides, Uncle's medicine bundle was taken from its place over his bed and set on a tripod behind the tent, and another bundle, painted with the same stripes as the hides, was hung there instead.

Shell Woman was there, and usually two or three of her sisters. If they helped Little Bear Woman, they had to be very careful, and if anyone made a mistake Shell Woman hit the place with her awl, gave a war whoop, and then picked out the sinew so the beads could be resewn.

"Why does she do that?" Mary asked.

"All women should pick out sewing mistakes. Cheyenne women are noted for their perfect work. Shell Woman can strike the error and give a war whoop like a man counting coup because she fought at the Sand Creek battle."

"What are all those hides for?"

"They are for the Sun Dance give-away. Now get busy and make some coffee and fry bread. Uncle will be back soon."

As the days grew shorter and then again longer, the pile of hides grew and grew. Four were specially beaded with the Sewing Women's stripe designs, and when they were finished Little Bear Woman gave a feast for the Sewing Women's Society, on the day before the Sun Dance. She stood beside the four hides, spread on the ground, with Shell Woman facing her across them, from the man's place at the west side of the tent.

"Daughter," Shell Woman began, "you and your cousins have worked long and hard on these skins. Now you shall have your reward. I am passing my power to you."

Bending forward, Shell Woman spread her hands over her feet and legs, and as she straightened herself drew the hands along her body to her heart. Little Bear Woman imitated the gestures. They drew their right hands along their left arms, and the left hands along their right arms, each time ending just above the heart. And at last Shell Woman drew both hands from the crown of her head downward, and held them out from her heart to Little Bear Woman's face, passing the power from the crown of Little Bear Woman's head and then downward, always directing it to the heart.

"There, Daughter," she said. "Now you are indeed Mah-hee-yuna, and shall be called that. When summer comes and you take the place of a wife to your unmarried brother in the Sun Dance, you will succeed. You will pass your brother's power through your body to your son."

Mary did not believe what she was hearing. Her mother, her own mother, who had taught her purity, could not—could *not*—be going to do this thing. Shell Woman must be mistaken. She turned and ran from the tent as fast as she could, and hid herself in the brush along the creek.

4

RUNNING AWAY

It was Minnie who finally found Mary, just at dusk. She dropped down on the ground and crawled under the bush where Mary was hiding, still face down.

"What you doing here?" Minnie demanded. "Everybody in camp is out looking for you. Don't you know that?"

"Let them look!" Mary retorted, but she rolled over and sat up. Her hair caught on the bush, and she jerked it free impatiently. "I'll never go back to camp again—never."

"Why not? It's home," Minnie said quietly.

"Not my home. I'm not Cheyenne anymore." Tears she had tried to hold back began to flow down her cheeks.

"You are too Cheyenne."

"Not anymore. I won't be."

"Well, why not?"

"Did you hear what my mother is going to do? At the Sun Dance?"

"Sure I heard. Everybody knows about it."

"I didn't. Not until today."

"It's a great honor. She will be a Sacred Woman—a Mah-hee-yuna."

"There's nothing sacred about it! Her own brother, and my brother."

"That makes her sacrifice even greater."

"Oh, you talk like an Indian!" Mary cried. "It's wrong. The old Cheyenne people teach us a woman must be pure. The missionaries tell us so. What's pure about this?"

"You can't stop it now—or any other time. They've already made their vows."

"Somebody could stop it!"

"Nobody could," said Minnie flatly. "You're too young even if you tried. Nobody would listen to you."

"Shell Woman could stop it. She's old, old. And she's a Mahhee-yuna. Everybody will listen to her."

"She won't have anything to do with it."

"I'll go to her. I'll ask her."

"Now?"

"In the morning. That's when you ask people for things, not when it's getting dark."

"Come home with me now," Minnie urged. "I'll get my brother to tell your mother where you are. In the morning we'll go to Shell Woman."

"All right," said Mary wearily. Her whole body ached. She got to her feet, and they went, hand in hand, back to Minnie's mother's tent.

The camp was full of bustle and excitement; although people were looking for Mary, nobody particularly noticed two young girls, or later, a younger boy, Minnie's brother, slipping through the darkness. When Minnie's brother returned, he handed Mary a cloth-wrapped bundle.

"Your mother sent it," he informed Mary. "She said you can't ask a favor of anybody without a present. These are for Shell Woman."

"Did you tell my mother what I was going to do?" Mary demanded.

"She made me tell her. I couldn't keep it a secret."

"What did she say?" Mary asked fiercely.

"She said it wouldn't do any good," the boy answered. "The vows were made a year ago. But she said the white part of you might think differently from the Cheyenne part."

"She said *that!* My own mother said that?"

"That's what she said."

"Take these back to her," Mary ordered. Tell her I will be all white from now on. Cheyennes are dirty!"

Minnie, who had spent the last few days carrying buckets of water and cleaning her mother's tent, shook her head.

"Don't say that, White Girl. You know it isn't true. Cheyennes keep themselves as clean as they can."

"Their minds are dirty."

"Well," inquired Minnie, always practical, "if you don't stay here, where will you go?"

Mary thought, and in her thinking slipped into sleep. In the morning she awoke knowing what she had to do.

To stay on at Darlington School was impossible. She might as well stay at home. Everybody knew her, and everybody would ask her questions. There was only one place to go. Johnny's Colony. She would be safe there, and Johnny would understand. He would certainly stop the Arapahoes from asking too many questions about Cheyenne things.

"I'm going away," she said to Minnie as they cleaned up after breakfast.

"Where?" Minnie inquired.

"If I tell you, will you keep it a secret?"

"Sure."

"I'm going to Johnny's Colony," Mary said in English, so no one else would understand if they overheard.

"He said no Cheyennes. Just Arapahoes."

"He'll take me," Mary said. "I'm not Cheyenne. My own mother said so to your brother. Promise you won't tell."

"I promise. But that's because I'm going with you," Minnie said, also in English.

"Why?"

"These old teachers here at Darlington are silly. They don't make sense. They talk all the time about being pure, but they get married and have babies themselves. They're just people, like the Indians. And they're not happy with each other. They don't yell and fight, but sometimes you see them not talk to each other for days."

"Johnny is always laughing," Mary said thoughtfully. "And he always talks to people even if he does not agree. That must be what people mean when they say 'love.' People should always get along together."

"Well, if you go to Colony, I will, too," Minnie insisted. "Now we have to make a plan. You can't go on a journey without planning." They had both slipped back into Cheyenne without noticing their change of languages.

"All right," Mary agreed. "We can put our clothes and extra moccasins in our shawls and make bundles to carry."

"We'll need food," Minnie reminded her. "We can take dried meat and some flour bread, and there's the river and some springs between here and there."

"Yes, we can get water. When shall we go?"

"Tomorrow night, when the first day's dancing is over and the dancers are resting."

From a distance the next morning, Mary watched her mother, stripped to the waist, enter the lodge, and her heart turned over inside her. She could hardly make herself watch, and she could not look away. She felt disgraced and proud at the same time.

That night, she and Minnie slipped out of the Sun Dance lodge into the darkness. She held onto Minnie's hand, and they went back to Mary's tent together to gather her few possessions.

And that night, again in the darkness, again hand in hand, they started for Seger Colony. When the moon was bleached bone-white, and there was a line of light in the east, they found a clump of plum bushes growing beside a spring and stopped. They ate and drank a little, and then slept. The ground was warm with summer's heat; when it cooled with dew, the girls awakened. They went on steadily through the bright heat of the day. It was hot, hot, but at last there was a downpour of rain to cool them. That night they found an abandoned shack where they could take off their dresses and hang them to dry. In the morning they went on, sure now that they would reach Johnny and the Colony.

By the end of the day they came over a little rise, and saw the cluster of buildings through the cottonwoods below them. Around the horizon stood the small knolls the Cheyennes called the Seven Sisters. These were sacred places, where men went to pray for power visions.

A path led down the rise, to the big trees in the valley below them. The path turned into a wagon road, which led directly to the main building. On its porch stood Johnny, puffing away at his cigar like a locomotive.

"Well," he said when he saw the two tired, bedraggled girls before him, "where did you come from?"

"Darlington. You know us," Mary answered.

"Why?" asked Johnny, and he blew a smoke ring. "There's a school for Cheyennes at Darlington."

"I'm not a Cheyenne," Mary said wearily.

"That's right, you're not," Johnny replied. "I'd forgotten. But what about Minnie here?"

"She's my sister-friend. She came with me."

"I see." Johnny looked them over again. "I guess the first thing to do is to feed you and give you a bath before we get word to your families."

"No!" Mary cried. "Not to mine. They aren't my family anymore. I want to stay here, with you. I won't go back to them! Anyway, my mother will know I'm here. I'm going to stay!"

"Like that, is it?" Johnny asked. He turned to Minnie. "What about you?"

Minnie stood thinking, then she shook her head slowly. "I want to stay here, but you can tell them that if you want to."

"Well, we can't do anything until morning," Johnny observed. "Maybe when you sleep on it you'll feel differently. Come on with me, now, to the kitchen, and we'll find you something to eat."

The Matron, Mrs. Bradley, was in the kitchen, putting away the last of the supper. She didn't say anything; just sat the girls down at a scrubbed wooden table and gave them bowls of beans from the school garden, cooked with salt pork, and slices of bread, and glasses of milk.

"Say your Grace," Johnny instructed them. They bowed their heads over the food and their lips moved in prayers of thanksgiving. Then they took up the enamel spoons the Matron had laid on the table and began to eat.

"Drink your milk," the Matron said when she saw that their glasses were untouched.

"We don't drink milk," Mary informed her. "Milk is for babies. We drink coffee, like other people."

"Everybody drinks milk here," Johnny said, and he poured himself a glass from the pitcher on the table and drank it. "If you stay here, you will have-to-drink-your-milk-at-every-single-meal." He spoke very sternly.

"Boys, too?" Minnie asked.

"Boys, too. It will make you all strong and healthy for the rest of your lives."

"I didn't know that," Mary said wonderingly. "I thought it was only for babies."

"Finish your supper, now," Johnny admonished them, "and then go with Mrs. Bradley and she'll show you the way to the girls' dormitory."

In the big room there was a row of cots, against each wall. The other girls were not in the room then; it was recreation time and they were downstairs playing. Many had gone home for the summer, so some of the beds had blankets and sheets on them and some were stripped to the mattresses. Mrs. Bradley first of all showed Mary and Minnie where the linen room was and how to take out their sheets and blankets, and she watched them make their beds. Then she gave them each a new dress and some underclothes, and led them down the hall to the bathroom. Each in turn, they climbed into the big tub, and Mrs. Bradley scrubbed them and washed their hair. Then she gave them white cotton nightgowns.

"You will take a bath and wash your hair every week, and more often if you have been doing dirty work," Mrs. Bradley said. She looked at a list that was pinned to the wall. "Mary on Monday, and Minnie on Wednesday. Those are good times. Put on your nightgowns now, and go to bed. The breakfast bell rings at seven, but there is a getting-up bell at six. You must be dressed and have your beds made and your part of the room cleaned up before breakfast."

Side by side, they lay on their cots as the room darkened.

"I smell funny," Mary whispered.

"It's that old yellow soap she washed us with," Minnie whispered back.

"I like the smell of yucca roots better, and they aren't any scratchier than that soap," Mary remarked.

The other girls came into the room then, with Mrs. Bradley.

"Everybody get into bed now," she told them, "and remember, no talking."

She blew out the lamp that hung from the rafters, and the big room was very quiet in the dark. It was strange to know there were people all around you and not hear them speaking. Not like a tipi. Not even like a tent.

5

COLONY SCHOOL

Within ten days their families came for them. Minnie's mother, father, and older brother were the first to ride up.

"We have come to take you home," Minnie's father announced.

"I don't want to go," answered Minnie. "I like it here. I'm learning a lot of things."

"I hope you're learning how to sew," Minnie's mother observed, looking her over. "Those clothes are too small for you. They're tight."

"That's because we drink our milk every day," Minnie informed her. "It makes us grow. Anyway, I work in the bakery, not the sewing room. Mary works there."

"Milk!" exclaimed Minnie's brother. "Milk is for babies. You're a grown woman. Pretty soon you'll be able to give milk yourself, if you have a baby."

"I'm not going to have a baby till after I get married," Minnie declared flatly. "Mrs. Bradley says it's wrong for girls not to get married first."

"Well, stay here if you want to be a white woman," her father said. "Come home with us if you want to be a Cheyenne."

"I'll stay," said Minnie, and nothing could make her change her mind.

It was even worse when Mary's uncle and Little Bear Woman came to get her.

"I am your mother's older brother," her uncle said quietly. "When I give you an order, you have no choice. I order you to come back to camp."

"Uncle, I must disobey you. If I stay here, I will be one of my father's people. Then you can't give me orders to do anything."

"Don't talk that way!" Little Bear Woman cried. "You know nothing about your father's people. They have thrown you away. Perhaps they do not know you were ever born. Come back to your own people, the Cheyennes."

Mary shook her head stubbornly. "I will come back someday, perhaps, but not until I know how my father's people live. I already know some of the things they believe. What you did at the Sun Dance was wrong, wrong, WRONG. You are a wicked woman and I don't want to live with you."

"So be it," said her uncle. He cut his horse with his four-thronged quirt and wheeled away. Little Bear Woman sat for a moment looking at Mary, and then she, too, turned and was gone.

Mary's own tears were falling. Mrs. Seger held her tightly until she was quiet. Then she said, "You won't regret this, I promise. It's better to know two ways of living than only one."

So Mary and Minnie stayed at the school at Colony. Mary worked in the sewing room, making dresses for the girls and suits for the boys. They had classes and exercises and evening hymn singing, and they had preachers on Sundays.

Johnny was building a church a little away from the school, to the west. He and some of the Arapaho men cut blocks of soft yellow sandstone from a bank near the river and hauled the material to the site he had chosen. Johnny would not use the red sandstone that was nearer. A church should be golden, he said.

Once Mary asked him if the church would have a regular preacher.

"Sure," said Johnny, blowing out a puff of smoke.

"What kind?" Mary asked. It seemed as if every preacher who came to the school belonged to a different church.

"Dutch Reformed Lutheran, of course," Johnny answered.

"We haven't had one of those," said Mary thoughtfully.

"I'm saving the best for the last," Johnny informed her. "Now get back to work and don't ask so many questions."

It seemed to Mary that there was no end to the questions she had to ask. Everything here was different—different even from

Darlington. Nothing was like the life she had lived before. Perhaps knowing that she had no home to go to on Saturdays had something to do with it.

In their own way, though, Sundays were exciting. The preachers usually came on Saturdays, and stayed with Johnny and Mrs. Seger. Johnny had built a guest room onto his house. He said anyone was welcome to stay in it, but nobody but the preachers ever seemed to.

On Sunday mornings they all had breakfast together in the school dining room. The preacher would say Grace before they could eat. Some of the Graces, like those the Presbyterian preacher said, were so long the food got cold. He was a Choctaw, and Johnny said Choctaws were always wordy people. The Kiowa Episcopal missionary, Joshua Givvens, said very short Graces.

Afterward the girls cleaned up the dishes while the boys pushed the tables back to the walls and lined up the chairs in rows. When everything was ready Johnny rang the school bell, and they all gathered for services.

You could forgive the Presbyterian minister for being wordy when he sang. His voice came pouring out like golden wild honey from a newly cut comb. Sometimes his wife sang with him, and the two voices joined and parted magically. His wife was a white woman. She had met her husband when he went east to study singing, and had chosen to return to the mission field with him. Mary's favorite of all their songs was "His Eye Is on the Sparrow." That was a fine thing for God to take care of all living creatures, like Maheo.

In some ways, the most interesting of all the preachers was the Baptist. He and his wife were Winnebagos, and Johnny often said he wondered how the Baptists ever got hold of them—they should have been Episcopalians, like Joshua.

They traveled in a hooded wagon, with a kitchen on the back, like a chuck wagon, and they lived in the wagon and often had their meals cooked by a young Negro servant, who rode horseback and looked after the wagon horses and did the camp chores. He always smiled, but he very seldom spoke. They called him "Boy," but he was a grown man. Johnny said it was un-Christian to treat him that way, but what could you expect from Baptists, who claimed their religion was older than Christianity anyway.

After the services, Johnny and his wife and the preacher and his wife and all the teachers went to Johnny's house and gossiped, while the boys set out the dining tables and chairs and the girls finished the noon dinner they had started cooking the day before. Sunday dinner was always chicken. Johnny said chicken and preachers went together.

On Sunday afternoon they had Bible School. Each child was given a Bible to read from, and passing out the Bibles was a great honor. You had to have no demerits from the previous week to be allowed to do it. Minnie was always in trouble for "borrowing" cookies from the kitchen, so she didn't pass out Bibles very often, but Mary sometimes did. She went down the girls' side of the room, handing them out, and one of the boys passed out Bibles to the boys.

One boy, who passed out Bibles about as often as Mary, was a Caddo named James Inkanish, whose parents lived near Binger. They had brought him and one of his cousins, Robert, to Colony because they did not like the Caddo school at Anadarko, and Johnny had broken his Arapaho rule for them, too, and he had kept the boys.

In Bible School the students did not have to be as stiff as they were in church. They could wiggle, and scratch their backs on the chairs. They even whispered sometimes. Johnny taught the Bible School himself. He said it was time for the Dutch Reformed Lutheran Church to get its licks in, and they might as well get used to it because they were all going to belong to that church when he got his missionary there.

In Bible School Johnny read a passage and then asked them what they thought it meant. They took turns answering. Some of the things in what he called the Old Testament were hard. Mary had never seen lions, and she didn't know why Daniel was supposed to be afraid of them. And Jael, pounding a tent stake through Sisera's head! Why would anyone want to do that? Mary knew what a tent stake was, all right. It was hard to pound into the ground, let alone going through a head bone, as hard as stone. Then there was Judith, who cut off a man's head! Mary and Minnie talked all these things over when they went outside to exercise—not play—between Bible School and Sunday night supper, which was usually bread and milk. "She was a real mean woman," Mary said about Judith. "As mean as a Sioux."

There was a girl in school whom the missionaries had named Judith, and they all watched her after that Bible lesson. You never knew when she might turn mean, like her namesake.

6

THE CHURCH

The stone church was finished at last, even to the backless wooden benches on which the congregation would sit, and the square table to hold the Bible. Mrs. Seger gave the Bible as her present to the church.

Now all the missionaries came at once for the dedication. It was like opening a woman's first tipi, Mary thought. Her mother had told her many times of the ceremonies that were held—how the old men smoked and prayed, how the women of the bride's family prepared and served a feast, and how the bridegroom's sisters carried the bride into the tipi on a blanket. She would have on new clothes, and her new moccasins would have beaded soles, so her feet should not touch the ground. She would be placed against a new, painted backrest, on her husband's right side. Then the newly married couple were left alone together, and life in the new tipi began.

Of course, nobody smoked at the church dedication, not even Johnny. Everyone wore new clothes, though, and Mary and the other girls in the sewing room had worked long and hard to make them. Some of the older boys had fitted the new uniforms of the others. A few of the tailors really liked the work and wanted to learn more about it, but others had just wanted to get out of work detail in the gardens and on the farm, or to have a chance to be with the girls. Their work was so poor Johnny made them do it over and over until it was about right. Even so, some of the uniforms looked pretty funny.

On the big Sunday they all marched from the school to the church. The preachers and their wives led the way; then came the teachers and the work trainers, and then the students. Mary and Minnie walked in the middle of the line. They were not very tall, and this time Johnny had assigned places by height, from the biggest to the littlest, so the line would look better.

Johnny was waiting on the porch, with the key to the church in his hand. He unlocked the door and threw the key as far as he could, into a clump of white ash trees.

"God's house should never be locked to anybody," Johnny said, and they all followed him inside.

It was a long service that Sunday. First the Reverend Joshua Givvens said the Lord's Prayer, and they all joined in. Then he read a prayer from a little black book he always carried, asking God to bless the church and everyone who worshipped there. Then he preached, and told them all of God's love for and welcome to all his children. It was a fine sermon and Mary enjoyed it, but then the Reverend Givvens prayed again, and she began to get tired.

She was relieved when the Presbyterian preacher stood up, but disappointed when he, too, prayed and preached. Mary began to wonder if the kettle of stewed chicken Minnie had left on the kitchen stove had boiled away or got cold. But then the Presbyterian minister sang "His Eye Is on the Sparrow," as if he knew the whole time what they all wanted him to do, and Mary was so happy she forgot about everything else but the song, and the voice that poured out, as golden as the stone walls of the church.

Then it was the Baptist preacher's turn. He said first, "God, bless this house and all who enter it." Then he turned to Johnny, who was sitting on the platform with the preachers. "John Seger, we thank you. You have done a great and good thing for these people, and for all of us, by giving us a house of worship. You and your good wife are the ones we truly bless this day."

He held out his open arms. "Sister Seger, do lead us all in singing 'Onward, Christian Soldiers!'" And as well as they could, they all sang the hymn.

Last of all, the Reverend Joshua Givvens made the sign of the cross in the air above them, and said the short blessing prayer with which he always ended his services. Johnny led the way, and they all trooped back to the school, leaving the church door standing open behind them.

When they got into the kitchen, Mary was happy to see that nothing bad had happened to the stewed chicken. She and the other older girls helped to serve food and put it on the tables. They rushed around, not only because they were hungry but because it felt good to move after all that sitting in church.

When dinner was over and the kitchen was clean and orderly, they went back to the church for Sunday School. This time Johnny's lesson was a short one, just the story of the miracle of the loaves and fishes.

"There is more than one kind of food," he finished. "The Reverend brought me a letter from the Dutch Reformed Lutheran Conference, which just met at Lake Mohonk, New York, and in a short time we will have our own preacher, Mr. Reese Kincaide. He will live here with us, so tomorrow morning we must get busy and build a house."

The house they built beside the church was of red sandstone and wood, and the wood was painted white. There was one big room in front, with two smaller ones behind it for a kitchen and bedroom.

"What do they want such a big front room for?" Minnie asked. Mary shook her head in puzzlement. Neither could imagine anyone's wanting a room that big unless the missionary planned to teach school there.

The day came when Johnny took the school buggy to the railroad at El Reno to meet the missionary and his wife. Jim Inkanish and Robert Cross followed Johnny with the wagon and team. When they came back, late in the evening, the wagon was loaded with furniture and trunks and big wooden boxes. Johnny and the missionary were talking, but the missionary's wife looked tired, as if she were about talked out.

That night the missionary family slept in the Seger guest room. In the morning, the work of unloading the wagon and dispersing its contents began.

All the trunks and wooden boxes were put in the front room, and the furniture in the two rooms at the back. They were pretty crowded, but the missionary and his wife were small people and didn't take up much room.

That night, after supper, Johnny made a speech to the students.

"Every church needs money," he said. "It has to have some way of earning its own way. So there is a word you can take to your mothers when you go home. We will go around ourselves and take it to the men.

"It is this. The people at Lake Mohonk have sent all the things in those boxes. There are knives and awls and beads. This church is for the Indians, and if the good beadworkers will come here, they can do beadwork to be sold. When it is sold, the women will be paid half the money it brings, and the rest will go to the church."

It was a new idea to the students. They knew that the officers and their wives at Fort Reno sometimes bought beadwork, but they had never thought that anyone else would. Mary put up her hand.

"Who will buy it?" she asked.

"People in the East," Johnny told her. "The Lake Mohonk Conference will sell it to them."

The services their own missionary, Mr. Reese Kincaide, held in the golden church were very simple.

First, the students and teachers marched in, singing. Sometimes they sang "Shall We Gather at the River?" and sometimes "I'm Washed in the Blood of the Lamb," and sometimes "He Walks with Me and He Talks with Me." They sang Christmas carols in the winter and Easter carols in the spring, and they always marched out, at the end of the service, singing "Onward, Christian Soldiers!"

In between, Mr. Kincaide read a passage from the Bible, and preached, and whoever wanted to stood up and prayed. Johnny and Mr. Kincaide must have talked together a lot when no one else was around, because the Bible passage and the preaching always fitted something that had happened at the school that week. Once in a while it would be something Mary thought no one but she and Minnie knew anything about. She didn't know how Mr. Kincaide found out.

They still had Sunday School in the afternoons, with Johnny as teacher, but now the lessons were more often from the New Testament than from the Old.

Mary liked the New Testament stories better. The people seemed kinder, somehow, except at the very end, where they were so mean to Jesus. And she didn't understand why His mother couldn't have had him born at home instead of going off somewhere and having to birth Him in a stable. She had heard her uncle say Indians didn't pay taxes, so why should those people? But the story about the donkey who wouldn't go to Damascus, and the woman who got mad at her sister for just sitting around, and Peter let down over the wall in a basket while the soldiers hunted for him—those were fine. Both Mary and Minnie began to like church better and better, now that they were really growing up.

7

MOHONK LODGE

Minnie took the word back to camp, and told the women about the beads at the church, and how they could sell things they made from them and get paid for their work.

Little Bear Woman called the Sewing Women's Society together in Shell Woman's tipi and they talked it over. Shell Woman lay on her bed, propped up with pillows stuffed with horsehair, and listened. When everyone had spoken, some supporting the idea and some opposing it, she said, "Listen to me. Times are changing. We women will have to change with them. I am too old to go to Colony, and too tired to do much work, but some of you should go and talk to this man. Then come back and tell me what his beads are like, and we will decide what to do. We must make our own decision."

Eight women went, finally, with Little Bear Woman leading them. When they arrived at the missionary's house, Mary was in the big room, helping Mrs. Kincaide unpack the boxes of supplies and set the smaller boxes that held the beads out on the tables.

It was the first time Mary had seen her mother since that day when Little Bear Woman had come to take her back to camp and she had refused to go. Her heart turned over inside her and then rose in her throat, choking her. She stood still, unable to move, and Little Bear Woman came to her daughter and put her arms around her.

"It's all right," she said quietly. "You will always be my daughter and I will always love you, no matter what you say. You are better off here, too, I think. Your skin is clear and pretty and you have grown taller. Let us forget what has happened in the past and go on together like good friends."

Tears rolled down Mary's face. She put her arms around her mother and hugged her, laying first one cheek and then the other against Little Bear Woman's. She could not speak, but she knew her mother understood why.

"Now, let us look at the beads," Little Bear Woman said.

Mrs. Kincaide stepped back from the table, and the Sewing Women looked it over.

"They are beautiful," Little Bear Woman said. "So fine and even, and such clear colors. It will be joy to work with these beads, and to get paid for it. . . ."

The women decided right away that they would take beads back to camp and make things with them. It took a long time for each of them to look at each strand of beads, and to decide what colors she wanted to use. Mostly they chose red, blue, and yellow, but there were different shades of each to be selected, as well as white and black beads, of course.

"What are you going to make?" Mrs. Kincaide asked Little Bear Woman, with Mary interpreting.

"I think I will make a bag," answered Little Bear Woman thoughtfully. "A long, narrow bag, like a pipe bag."

"Why not make one like this?" Mrs. Kincaide asked, and opened a magazine. It had a whole page of bag designs, and she pointed to one that was flat and square.

"Cheyennes don't make bags that shape," Little Bear Woman remarked thoughtfully.

"Can't you try?" asked Mrs. Kincaide. "White women like to carry bags like that, and it will be a new way to work."

Little Bear Woman still looked doubtful, but she took the beads. "I have a buckskin and sinew at home," she said.

"We will pay you for whatever you use of your own," Mrs. Kincaide assured her.

"What do they call this place?" one of the other women asked.

Mr. Kincaide had come into the room, and was listening and watching. None of the women had even noticed him, they had been so interested in the beads. Later, Mary learned that he always walked as quietly as if he wore moccasins instead of shoes, although he never did.

"I think we will call it Mohonk Lodge, after the conference that made it possible," he answered thoughtfully. And Mohonk Lodge it was, ever after.

When the women brought their work back, all coming together again, Mr. Kincaide did a surprising thing. He got out a big ledger book, like the one the trader kept accounts in at the store, but with blank, unruled pages. He carefully measured each piece of work the women brought him, and he drew its designs and colors on a page of the book, with the woman's name and the date.

"Why are you doing that?" Mary asked him.

"So we will have a record of what kind of work is most popular," said Mr. Kincaide. "That way, we can make more like it. These designs will be known as Mohonk designs."

Mary was shocked. Every woman had her own designs, and she did not even share them with her sisters in the Sewing Women's Society. Only the most sacred designs of the Sewing Women's Society were used over and over. Mary could hardly tell her mother what Mr. Kincaide had said.

"That is wrong," said Little Bear Woman, and the other women said "Nah!" and shook their heads in disapproval. Some of them even reached for their work, to take it back.

"What's the trouble?" Mr. Kincaide asked.

"I guess you don't know much about Indians," Mary remarked. "We don't use each other's designs. Ever."

"But if some designs sell better than others, we would get more money if more women made them," Mr. Kincaide protested. "If each woman kept her own designs, then the women whose designs did not sell would have nothing. It would not be fair.

"Tell them this for me, Mary," the missionary continued. "As long as they work for Mohonk Lodge, they will be given beads only for Mohonk Lodge designs. Beads for other things they will have to buy, the way they would at the trader's. But if one of them brings me a new design that I like and it sells well, I will make it a Mohonk design. Then I will give them beads to make it. In that way our design book will grow."

Mary stonily interpreted. The women put their work down, slowly.

"We have too little to feed our children," Little Bear Woman remarked sadly. "Our old people go hungry, too. Our men have nothing to hunt, and they don't know how to farm. It's up to us to take care of our families. We will use Mohonk Lodge designs."

When Mary finished interpreting what her mother said, she added, "It's a bad thing to do to them. Something bad will happen."

"Don't be silly," Mr. Kincaide snapped. "That's just Indian superstition, Mary. You go to church and Sunday School. You know better than that."

Mary hung her head and did not answer. It was to be many years before she found out how right she was.

Mohonk Lodge soon became a gathering place for Cheyenne and Arapaho women. They came in groups to collect their money, get more beads, and watch Kincaide make his careful copies of designs. Each time a particular design was sold, Mr. Kincaide marked a score on the bottom of the sheet where it had been drawn, and the women began to look through the book for the designs with the most scores. When they had memorized them, they copied the popular designs in their own beadwork, perhaps changing the arrangement of colors a little, and brought them back to be sold.

Some of the older girls at Colony began to spend time at Mohonk Lodge, too. Johnny let them take their recreation time there in bad weather, and in that way they saw more of their mothers, and learned more from them, than they had in a long time. Mothers brought buckskin and sinew for their daughters to work with. As time went on, and buckskin got harder to get as the deer grew scarcer, Mr. Kincaide sent away for a soft leather he called suede. At first he ordered only buckskin color, but one day he opened the package all sorts of colors tumbled out: skins dyed rose, blue, and beautiful golden yellow. Some were even dark blue or green, and a few were black.

"Ah!" said all the women in the room; they were delighted as well as surprised. The beadwork they did on the colored leather sold even better than buckskin, though the suede was harder to work with. Sewing on buckskin, a woman could slip her awl between the two layers of skin, so only the beads on the outside showed and the inside stitches were hidden. Suede was too soft and thin to sew like that, and would not split, so the inside stitches showed. They were tiny, and only another Indian woman, probably, would have noticed them, but the women knew they were there.

Sometimes a woman came in with her own hide, to buy beads to make moccasins for her husband or son. Then Mr. Kincaide would measure with his hands the amount of buckskin she needed for the uppers of that pair, and trade her beads for the rest of the hide. He measured with the flat palms of his hands, as the women did, and none of them could measure better.

Because of the Lodge, Mary saw more of her own mother. She still could not understand—and she had been taught not to forgive—what her mother had done, but they became friends again.

"How is Shell Woman?" she asked one day, as they sat side by side on the floor sewing. She suddenly realized that she had not heard the old lady spoken of for many months.

"That one has left us," Little Bear Woman answered. Like all the older women, she would not speak the name of the dead. To do so might bring the spirit back to haunt her. "She was very old and very tired," Little Bear Woman continued. "She had lived a long life—longer than most people. I think she was glad to go over the hill and join her loved ones on the other side, as the Arapahoes say. There were more people she knew there than here, at the end."

Mary sighed. Like her mother, she did not mourn the old lady outwardly, but she knew she would miss her teacher always.

"I think my brother will be the next to go," Little Bear Woman went on. "He is almost as old as she was, and now he has the white man's coughing sickness, like Joshua Givvens."

Mary shivered. She and the other older students had been warned that the Episcopal minister was ill and they must not go too close to him. They had watched him grow thinner and paler as time went on, and after the church dedication he stopped coming to Colony. Some of the girls had whispered that Reverend Givvens was jealous because Johnny had built a church for others, but Mary did not believe that. She had seen people with the coughing sickness in the camp all her life, and she knew that a time came when they could not speak because it made them choke.

"I think you had better come home this summer," said Little Bear Woman quietly. "I will need you, with your uncle sick. It is time for you to take a share of your family's problems, even though you say you do not belong to us. You are a woman now. You can't stay in school always unless you want to be a teacher. Think about it."

"When will you come back?" Mary asked.

"When I finish these moccasins for your uncle." She held them up, and Mary saw she was beading the rawhide soles for the feet of the dead, which would never walk the earth again.

Mary's mind was made up. "I will come back to you in the summer," she promised.

That night she told Johnny what her mother had told her. He listened quietly, his face veiled in cigar smoke, while she spoke.

"I thought you wanted to be a teacher," he said when Mary finished.

"I do. I do want to! But just one summer at home when my mother needs me. . . ."

"You'll never be anything but a Cheyenne," Johnny said. "Go, for this summer, anyway. You can always come back. It might be the best thing. That Inkanish boy will be here for the summer, and he's been making sheep's eyes at you, as it is."

"What are sheep's eyes?" Mary asked, and Johnny laughed, saying, "You'll know soon enough."

Mary watched Jim closely after that, but his eyes looked just the way they always had: plain brown, with the beginnings of smile wrinkles at the corners. Not at all like a sheep's. But he was around where she was a good deal, whenever he could get off work detail; even Mrs. Seger said he followed her like Mary's little lamb.

Robert Cross tagged after Minnie the same way. The two boys were always together, as the two girls were, and Mrs. Seger said jokingly they ought to make a dancing square for graduation.

When Minnie's mother and father came for her at the end of school, they brought a spare horse for Mary.

"Your mother really needs you," was all that Minnie's mother said.

When Mary got home, she saw that it was true. Now the family had moved into a square wooden frame house, and Mary's uncle lay on his bed in one of the rooms. He looked as if he were already dead, and Little Bear Woman was thin and tiny and tired from taking care of him.

"Good," she said to Mary when the girl slid down from her horse. "I do need you."

All summer long, while her mother fed and washed and nursed the sick man, Mary took care of the house. She finished the moccasins with beaded soles that her mother had begun.

8

COURTING

Jim Inkanish drove into the yard one day late in the summer, with his father's team and wagon.

"I came to help out," he told Mary when she went out to meet him. "You need a man around this place."

And so he stayed. He helped Mary with the housework and he took over the cooking. Most Caddo men were good cooks, and Jim had worked sometimes in the kitchen at Colony School. He helped Little Bear Woman care for the sick man, too. He went for the Government doctor when they could do no more themselves.

The doctor shook his head when he saw his patient. "Even if you had sent for me earlier, I couldn't have done anything more than you have. Keep him clean, make him eat when he will, and let him rest." He looked around the room, scrubbed as clean as sand and water could get it, the windows tightly closed and a pile of used rags by the sick man's bed. "Two more things you can do," the doctor said. "Open all the windows, day and night. When he gets cold, cover him, but don't close the windows. And take a pair of sticks, like tongs, and pick up all those rags and burn them. Burn the rags he uses every time, from now on."

"But what is on those rags is part of him," Little Bear Woman protested. "How can we burn it while he is still alive?"

"To open the windows will let the sickness fly around, all over the house," said Mary, supporting her mother.

"The house is full of sickness now," said the doctor sternly. "To keep it indoors makes more danger for the rest of you!"

"I'll do it," Jim offered. "I'm another tribe. Thomissey taught us things like this."

"Thomissey? Do you mean Thomas C. Battey, the missionary who had the school at Anadarko?" the doctor asked. "He must have been a great man. I wish I could have known him."

"He went away, back to Iowa, where he came from," Jim said. "But he taught the Caddos a lot of things before he left."

After the doctor went away, Jim picked up the rags and burned them on a pile of cedar branches in the yard. He built the fire so the wind blew the cedar smoke toward the house, to purify it and everybody in it.

Then Jim worked all day to open the bedroom windows Little Bear Woman had nailed shut. It was a corner bedroom, and the wind blew through it gently, so the air in the room felt clean and fresh.

Even without the Indian doctor, who said he didn't know how to cure white men's sickness; even without any medicine from the Government doctor, uncle seemed to get better for a while. Then, one night, Mary felt her mother shaking her foot gently to waken her.

"Go and get Jim," Little Bear Woman commanded. "I need him."

Mary had slept in her clothes all summer, changing them in the morning, because this just might happen. Now she ran, barefoot, out to the arbor where Jim was sleeping and took hold of his foot. She must have shaken him harder than she meant to, because he sat up at once and gaped at her.

"What is it? What's happened?" he asked, wide awake at once.

"He's worse," Mary answered. "Hitch up, and go for the doctor."

Jim gave her a hug. Mary was surprised. Their eyes had met and crossed sometimes during that summer, but she only thought of Jim as a good friend. She gasped, and pushed him away.

"Go on," she ordered. "*Hurry,* or it may be too late."

And when Jim got back with the doctor, it was too late. Uncle lay stretched on his bed, his face covered with red clay.

"What now?" Little Bear Woman asked. "In the old days we would have burned the bedding and given away all his clothes. . . ."

"Only sensible Indian custom I ever heard of," snapped the doctor. "But you listen to me. Burn everything, not just the bedding, but the clothes—everything."

"And put him naked into the ground, without anything to keep the earth from him?" Mary cried.

"You can get a clean new blanket for him and wrap him in it," the doctor said. "Then bury the blanket with him."

"How can we get clean new blankets? We have no money," Little Bear Woman said. Jim's hand on her arm stopped her.

"I am the man here now," Jim said. "It's up to me to see my friends are buried right." Motioning toward the wagon and the tied horses, he said to the doctor, "You want a ride back to town? You can come with me, or I'll drive in and bring your riding horse back here."

"I'll come with you," the doctor answered. "There's nothing I can do here any more."

"Nothing," said Mary bitterly. "And nothing you have done, that I can see."

The doctor shook his head. "Nothing anybody knows how to do," he said sadly. "Quiet, rest, fresh air—that's what kept him alive this long."

When the men had gone Little Bear Woman and Mary built a fire of cedar branches in the yard, where the wind blew away from the house so it could take Uncle's spirit away. They brought out clothing and rolled Uncle's body from side to side to pull the mattresses from beneath him.

Mary noticed her uncle's medicine bundle hanging above his bed, and reached for it.

"Don't touch it!" Little Bear Woman cried fiercely. "Don't burn it! I am the only one left who has the right to do that. Those power things, they can hurt you if you handle them."

It seemed to Mary as if something *had* hurt her—just as badly as she could be hurt. Perhaps the power bundle had punished her because she had run away to school. Or perhaps she had been hurt by the white doctor, with the medicine he admitted wouldn't heal. Whatever it was, her heart felt heavy inside her. She left the bundle where it was, and followed her mother out of the house. She watched in the gathering dusk while her mother shook loose her hair and sprinkled it with ashes. Then Little Bear Woman slipped her big skinning knife from its sheath, gashed her arms and legs, and let the blood fall on the fire until it went out.

Startled though she was by what she had seen, Mary let down her own long school braids and unplaited them. In her turn, she reached for the skinning knife. Her mother jerked it away.

"Not you!" she exclaimed. "That is for older women, who have borne children. They can mourn that way."

She looked at Mary sharply. "Just what is Jim to you?" she demanded.

"He's my friend. My good friend. We go for walks on the school ground together sometime. And he came here to help us."

"Let it stay that way," Little Bear Woman said. "We owe him thanks for helping us when we needed help, but I don't owe him you."

Johnny came a few days later, driving up in the school wagon.

"You two young'uns better come back," he said. "Load up what you can in your wagon. And you come on with me too, Minnie," he said to Little Bear Woman. "Your other daughter and your brothers are gone. It isn't good for you to stay here alone, right now. You can give Mrs. Seger a hand in the girls' dormitory, maybe do some beadwork at the Lodge; see your girl whenever you want to. Tell her, Mary."

Mary interpreted.

"I will come," Little Bear Woman assured them. "This is a haunted place for me now, and not safe to stay in. Wait till I get something." She turned back into the house, and came out with a long, cloth-wrapped bundle in her arms.

"That's all?" Johnny asked. "No clothes?"

"She has to buy cloth and make new ones," Mary explained. "It's how she shows her sorrow."

"All right, if she wants to," Johnny said. "I've been thinking, Mary. You and Jim here are old enough to work at the school. You can still have some classes, but we'll put you in the sewing room and Jim on the farm, and you can both be learning at the same time you're working."

"All right," Mary said. And so it was arranged. They were all together at the school, as they had been during the summer, but she and Jim didn't see as much of each other as they had before.

How it happened, Mary was never quite sure. One day she and Jim were just good friends, and the next day, suddenly, they couldn't see enough of each other and didn't want to see anyone else, not even their friends Minnie and Robert. It was as if they belonged together, and needed nobody.

Little Bear Woman watched them for about a week, and then she said, "Tell him to send his family to me."

Jim's sister, Alice, was enrolled at the school, and Mary went to her. They were good friends. Alice had had her English name before she came, and Johnny had never changed it. Alice she was, among all the Marys and Minnies and Marthas.

"My mother wants to speak to yours," Mary informed her.

"All right," Alice agreed. "I'm going home this Saturday. I'll tell her."

With Alice as her spokeswoman, Mary felt better. This was doing it the right way; the old way. Uncle would have approved. She went back to Little Bear Woman.

"Alice will tell them," she said.

On Monday the Inkanish family arrived in their farm wagon: Jim's mother and father, his two older brothers, and the brothers' wives. They all went together to Johnny's office, and Little Bear Woman wrapped up her beadwork in an old clean towel Mary had found in the kitchen and joined them.

"I think I know what you've come for," Johnny said. "One boy and one girl. Is that right?"

"That's right," Jim's father said. "One boy and one girl."

"Well," said Johnny, "I know you don't know exactly how old they are, but I'd say they were in their early twenties. They're old enough."

He spoke to Alice, who had slipped into the room quietly. "Go and get them," Johnny ordered. "Let's see what they have to say." Alice went out as quietly as she had come in.

When Mary entered, her mother held out her arms to her and kissed her lightly on each cheek. "I told you I didn't owe him you," she whispered, "but I guess I do. He's a good boy. Be happy." She turned her back on Jim and spoke to his mother. "I may not speak to him until I make him certain presents," she said. "When I have done that, he will be like my own son to me."

Jim's mother nodded. "We know about that Cheyenne custom," she said. "Our ways are different. But as long as we both have good children, we don't have to worry about other things. Let them be happy."

Jim's father spoke up. "Sister-in-law," he said to Little Bear Woman, "we have no horses to give them in the old way. What we have is a house on Caddo land, and since we have moved to Anadarko, I will give it to them. A house lasts longer than horses, the white people say."

"Thank you," said Mary.

A house! A house of their own! That was the greatest thing she had learned at Colony: She wanted a house, where she could feed and care for a family. She felt shy, suddenly. She had broken the Cheyenne rules and spoken to her father-in-law. Mary looked fearfully at Little Bear Woman, but her mother smiled and nodded, and she knew it was all right.

"You don't mind if she's half white?" Little Bear Woman asked Jim's mother.

"We don't mind. She's half Indian, even if it's another tribe."

"That's settled, then," Johnny said, getting up. "We can have the wedding in the church next Wednesday. Wednesday's a lucky day for a bride. Robert Cross and Minnie want to get married, too. We can have a double ceremony. Mr. Kincaide will arrange to have the Presbyterian minister here. He will be glad to let him use our church." Everyone was pleased, since they all knew and liked the Presbyterian minister.

Then it was all hustle and bustle and dressmaking and getting ready. In the old days it would have been different; they would have had to make tipis for the brides and grooms and new buckskin clothing. The families would have exchanged horses.

On Wednesday they walked to the church, Mary and Minnie in white dresses and each wearing a veil, Jim and Robert Cross in new blue serge suits.

After the Presbyterian minister performed the wedding ceremony, Mr. Kincaide led the way back to the school dining room, and they had what Mrs. Seger called "a reception." The two young couples stood in line with their parents and Mr. and Mrs. Kincaide and Johnny and Mrs. Seger. Everyone walked by them and shook hands with them. The older people blessed them, and some who could pressed money into the girls' palms.

Then it was over, and Mary and Jim could leave for their new home, west of the present-day town of Binger. Minnie and Robert Cross were going to stay at Colony. Robert would work at the school, and Johnny had given them a little house to live in. Mary went up to the room she shared with her mother to change out of her white dress and into a blue calico one.

"What are you going to do?" she asked her mother. She was suddenly startled to realize she had forgotten her mother; she had been so busy thinking about herself.

"I'll stay here," Little Bear Woman answered. "I can keep on working as long as I want to, Johnny says."

"Won't you come and live with us?"

"Not till I make moccasins and tipi furnishings and a saddle blanket for my son-in-law. You know the Sewing Women's Society's rules. I have no right to speak to your husband or to live in your house until I have done that. They are very special and they must be made after the marriage. It will take a long time, I'm afraid. I'll need a lot of beads."

Mary thought of the money she had just received, which was now piled on the dresser. Half of it belonged to Jim, but half of it was hers. She carefully counted and divided silver and bills into two piles, then picked up one and gave it to her mother.

"Here," Mary said. "You can buy some of your beads with this."

"Eight dollars!" Little Bear Woman said, counting it. "That's a lot of money. It was given to you for what you need. You can't give it all away."

"Only half of it," Mary replied. "See, here's Jim's half. I won't touch his. But I guess I need my mother as much as anything in the world."

"You're just a little girl," Little Bear Woman said, tears rolling down her cheeks. "Just a little girl, and I let you get married."

Mary drew herself up straight. She wanted to cry, too, but she didn't.

"I'm a grown woman now," she said. "I have a husband. Now we can try to take care of you." Quickly, before her mother could see she was crying, Mary ran from the room.

Then they were in Jim's father's wagon, loaded with their clothes and some new pots Mrs. Seger and Mrs. Kincaide had gone together to give them, and Jim picked up the lines. Everybody was laughing and talking and crying a little, because they would be missed at the school.

Driving away from Colony with a man—even with Jim—was strange. Mary could not get used to the thought that she had married this man; this was the man she had married forever, in the eyes of God and the people. She wondered how they would manage certain things. Living in her mother's house, Jim had cooked for everybody, and now she didn't remember how he liked his coffee! And she didn't know whether he'd want a sweat bath, or go swimming, or what.

Well, she'd find out. Caddos were different, anyway.

9

MARRIAGE

Being married was strange, but Mary began to remember without trying how Jim did things, and how he liked them. In fall there was little fieldwork to do, and Johnny wanted Jim to come back to Colony and work in the carpenter's shop. But Jim decided to do his carpentry at home. The house had stood empty since Jim's parents had moved to Anadarko, and even though Jim's mother and Alice had scrubbed and cleaned it before the wedding, there was still work to be done. Boards had blown loose from the studs at the side of the house, and Jim began nailing them back firmly. He took his share of the wedding-present money to the trading post, for nails and other supplies; he even got some paint for the inside of the house. While he worked outside, Mary painted her kitchen white, the bedroom blue, and the living room pale pink. She would have liked nice bright yellow instead of the pink, but these were the colors Jim had brought, and she used them. A white kitchen was all right; it reminded her of the inside of a new tipi, before the smoke darkened the walls. Besides, all the kitchens she had ever seen, at Colony, were painted white. But the blue made her feel sad, for some reason, and she never had thought much of pale pink as a color—too washed-out.

It was a funny little house, after the great barn of a dormitory at Colony. Mary had no trouble keeping it clean and in order. There was even a slate sink in the kitchen, and Jim kept her water buckets well filled morning and evening.

In the evenings they sat by the painted globe lamp in the living room and talked. Jim complained that the lamp did not give as much light as a lantern, and used more kerosene, but Mary thought the lamp was too beautiful not to use. Sometimes they had company. Alice, who had just married, and her husband, Robert Cussen, would drive over in their buggy from the adjoining farm, or Jim's father and mother might come up from Anadarko, about twenty miles south. Sometimes Mary and Jim went visiting in their turn. A lot depended on the weather and the amount of farm work that had to be done.

Every Saturday, without fail, they hitched the team to the wagon and drove into Binger. There was always a little shopping to be done, and at the same time they saw all their friends and neighbors. People took their lunches and shared them from one wagon to the next, and everybody laughed and gossiped and had a good time.

Sundays Mary and Jim tried to go to Colony to church, but sometimes the roads were too bad. Then they stayed at home and read the Bible; Jim prayed for both of them. Once he even tried to preach a sermon, seriously modeling himself on Mr. Kincaide, but this was so funny that Mary began to laugh. She laughed until her sides hurt. And Jim gave up sermons.

"I tell you," he said, "I think sermons are all right in church, but at home we need another kind of teaching, like in the old days."

So after that they sat on Sunday mornings and talked about the ways their different peoples did things, and why, and how.

Mary woke up feeling sick one Saturday morning. Her head ached and she was too dizzy for a while to get out of bed. Jim brought her some coffee, but she couldn't stand the smell of it and asked him for a cup of plain water. Even that she threw up, but she felt better afterward.

"Maybe we shouldn't go to town today," Jim said.

"I'll be all right," Mary replied. "It will do me good to get outdoors. And I want to go to the grocery and get some of those big round white hardtack crackers. I feel as if I could eat a barrel of them."

They met Jim's mother in the store, while Mary was buying a whole pound of crackers.

"I thought you didn't like those," Jim's mother said.

"I just got hungry for them," Mary explained. "Do you want one?"

"No," her mother-in-law replied. "If you're that hungry for them, you'd better eat them all."

Mary took a hardtack cracker out of the bag and ate it, shamelessly, standing there in the store. She knew that neither her mother nor Mrs. Seger would think it was very nice of her. They believed in eating at mealtimes, and not just when you were standing around. But Mary wanted that cracker so much! So she ate it, and then she ate another.

Jim's mother kept watching. "How long have you felt this way?" the older woman asked.

"I just woke up like this today," Mary replied.

Minnie's mother came into the store.

"Good morning," Mary said. "Would you like a cracker?" She held out the sack, while munching her third hardtack.

"Not that way," Minnie's mother said. "I don't like them except with soup."

"Neither do I, usually," Mary said between bites.

Minnie's mother and Mrs. Inkanish exchanged looks. Then Minnie's mother made a loop in front of her, as if her belly were swollen, and began to rock her arms as if she held a baby in them. Mrs. Inkanish nodded. Mary could feel herself blush all over, to see them both rocking imaginary babies in the middle of the grocery store.

"That's all that's the matter with you," Minnie's mother said. "You're going to have a baby. Women get like that beforehand. When Minnie was coming, all I wanted was dried meat. All the time. Nothing else. It's natural."

"Oh," said Mary. The explanation had not occurred to her before, even though she knew it was true.

"All right," Mary said. It suddenly seemed to her that she wanted to see her mother more than anything in the world.

Next day, when Little Bear Woman heard the news, she did not seem surprised. "It's soon," she said, "but you will have been married just a year when the baby is born. Nobody can talk about you and Jim."

"What would they say?" Mary asked.

"Oh, you know as well as I do how people talk," Little Bear Woman told her. "If you had your first baby too soon, they might say you had been a bad girl, and you and Jim had been hiding in the bushes to get the little one started."

"We didn't!" Mary exclaimed.

"I know you didn't," said Little Bear Woman, "but you'd be surprised at what some people will say sometime."

She sat looking at her daughter, and nodded. "I'd say about fall," she said. "Now, listen to me. I'm going to tell you the things you can do and the things you can't do. I'll come and stay with you when the baby is born, but I can't be there all the time yet.

"Now, listen to me. You'll have to make your husband sleep in another bed, and don't have anything to do with him until a month after the baby is born. That's the most important of all. It's hard on the man, but it proves he *is* a man, and has respect for his wife.

"Another rule is that you must not eat sausages, or anything that has a covering on it. Don't eat any of those noodles that Mrs. Seger is always serving. In fact, don't eat anything that is stringy. The baby is fastened to you by a cord, and you don't want it to get strangled. If you eat anything stringy, the cord can get twisted around its little neck."

"Can I go on eating crackers?" Mary asked.

"As long as they taste good to you," her mother assured her. "Time will come when you won't want them, but that's a long way off now. Just be careful about stringy things.

"Take a sweat bath every four days. Be sure you keep yourself clean and make your husband do the same thing."

"Do I have to jump in the creek after I sweat?" Mary asked. She suddenly felt as if she could not stand the cold water.

"It will be better for you if you do," her mother said, "but right at first you don't have to. In warm weather, though, you most likely will want to.

"Don't look at ugly things, if you can help it. Don't help with the butchering; leave that to the men. Think about beautiful things: the things Maheo made. Think about how beautiful your baby will be, to make it healthy."

"Will it be a boy?" Mary asked.

"Only Maheo and the Spider Grandmother, who watches over all women, know that," said Little Bear Woman. "None of the rest of us will know until the baby is born. Pray only that you have a healthy child."

Mrs. Seger instructed Mary, too.

"Get some clothes ready for the baby," she said. "You want it to look nice. I have some flannelette in the storeroom that I'll give you. You can start hemming diapers."

It seemed to Mary that she had never stitched so many hems in her life, even when she worked in the sewing room. Mrs. Kincaide gave her more flannelette, to wrap the baby in, and Minnie and Alice made little shirts and dresses out of whatever cloth they had.

Mary gave up her white-woman's-style school dresses. They were about worn-out anyway, and now she was outgrowing them. Only her white wedding dress she put away; the others she cut up for baby clothes. If the baby should be a girl—and she greatly hoped it would be—someday her daughter would need a white wedding dress, too. So Mary began to wear the straight-up-and-down calico dresses, cut like old-fashioned buckskin dresses, because they were loose and comfortable. Little Bear Woman made them with open sleeves, in the true Cheyenne style.

"That way you can nurse your baby without uncovering yourself," she said.

So Mary dressed like a Cheyenne mother, and as the months passed, she began to look more and more Cheyenne. She let her hair hang in long braids, because it was too much work to pile it on top of her head. She wore moccasins instead of shoes, because they rested her feet. Jim was well pleased with the change.

"You look like a real Indian," he told her.

"Only my eyes," Mary answered. "You don't think the baby will have light eyes, do you?"

"What does that matter?" Jim countered. "We'll still love it."

Only the baby's cradle worried Mary. She spoke to her mother about it.

"If I get the beads, and some pretty leather from Mr. Kincaide, do you think the Sewing Women's Society would make it?" she asked. "Alice doesn't know how to make a Cheyenne cradle."

"Don't go near any of the Sewing Women except me!" Little Bear Woman exclaimed. "That would put a curse on everybody, if this baby's a boy. I'll see about the cradle."

Mary was in her ninth month when she saw Minnie and Little Bear Woman coming up the lane. They must have worked very hard, she thought. They had a loaded horse—a saddle horse—and on its back were a saddle blanket, a pair of moccasins, two saddlebags, a bedspread, and pillow covers, all made in the Sewing Women's Society's stripes. From the pommel of Minnie's saddle hung a great old-fashioned horseback cradle, decorated with marching deer around the hood. It was the most beautiful cradle Mary had ever seen, and she hugged Minnie and told her so.

"You are my sister," was all Minnie said.

Jim continued sleeping on a couch in the living room. He carefully folded his bedding and the cot every morning, and put them away, so the room would look nice.

Little Bear Woman shared the bedroom with Mary at first, while Jim and Robert Cussen started building another room for her, off the kitchen.

"You'll have your own tipi again," Mary teased her mother.

There were only a few more days to wait.

Mary woke with a shock of pain one morning, and clutched her mother's arm. "It's coming, it's coming!" she cried.

"Get up," Little Bear Woman commanded, and walked her to the little hut away from the house which Mary had used during her menstrual periods. Little Bear Woman had it all clean and fresh, with white sand strewn on the floor. She brought the sand from the river herself, one bucketful at a time, so Jim wouldn't have to have any part of the work on this lodge.

There was a bed of sage, thicker even than a Sun Dance bed, with old quilts spread over it, but Little Bear Woman would not let her daughter lie down for a long time. Instead, they walked and walked, around and around the outside of the hut, from the east to the south, to the west, to the north, and paused to draw a breath, and walked again, while the sun rose to mid-sky and started down the west.

At last Mary had had all she could stand. "Let me lie down,

Mother," she begged, and Little Bear Woman led her into the hut. Even then she did not let Mary lie down. She had dug a hole in the middle of the floor and set two upright poles on its east side. She made Mary kneel over the white sand with which she had lined the hole and grasp a pole firmly in each hand.

"Pull," Little Bear Woman ordered. "Pull as hard as you can."

Between the pulling and the pain Mary was wringing wet with sweat. She hardly knew that Minnie and her mother had come into the hut until she felt Minnie's strong arms around her, pulling backward and pressing down at the same time, and she heard Minnie's mother cry, "There it is! There's its little head!"

Mary fell over backward on the sand. Little Bear Woman and Minnie undressed her, and bathed her with warm water, bandaged her, and put clean clothes on her. Little Bear Woman tipped spoonfuls of warm broth into her mouth and then Minnie appeared, a bundle in her arms, and held it out to Mary.

"Here is your son," Minnie said. "If you want to give him to me, I'll take him. I don't think I'll ever have any of my own."

"Oh, yes, you will," Minnie's mother said comfortingly. "You're impatient, that's all." She laid back the wrappings and studied the little body carefully. "Perfect," she said. "A beautiful little boy. Aren't you happy, Vee-hay-kah? He's all Indian."

Mary rewrapped the baby and clutched him to her. Almost all Indian, anyway, she thought. The baby felt strong and firm in her arms. She hugged him to her fiercely.

"Give him to me for a moment," Minnie's mother said. "Let me show him to his father and the world. Later I'll pierce his ears and give him his name."

Mary was so tired she was slipping into sleep when Minnie's mother came bringing the baby and laid him in her arms again. He was in his night cradle now, a plain tube of rawhide that was laced up the front with a buckskin cord and had a flap at the back to support his head.

"Now you can sleep," said Little Bear Woman, "and when you wake, you can tend him."

Mary stayed in the hut four days. It seemed to her that she and the baby never had a moment alone together. She called him George.

Women came and went, bringing presents for Mary and the baby. All the Sewing Women were there, at different times. They told Mary they would make her one of them when she was ready. Mrs. Seger and Mrs. Kincaide came, with more flannelette. Mary was beginning to understand why they gave her so much of it.

On the morning of the fifth day, Little Bear Woman wakened her before sunrise. "Come out, now," she instructed, and Mary crawled through the low doorway with George in her arms and stood facing the sun while it rose.

The world was very fresh and clear that fall morning. White ash glowed red and danced among the other trees. Jim came from the house, and held out his arms for his son. Together the three passed through the kitchen door and to the table where Little Bear Woman had breakfast ready for them.

Two days later, when George was a week old, Mary found the stump of his navel cord in his diaper when she was changing him. Excited, and a little frightened, she called her mother. "That's good," said Little Bear Woman. "I have the case ready for it."

And she brought Mary a little beaded turtle, red and black.

"Hang it on the head of his cradle," she told Mary. "That is part of the afterbirth, which is the other half of the child. He must keep it always, to be a whole man. When he grows older, you can put it away for him."

10

THE MOVE

The first few years of the 1900's were hard ones for farmers. There was little rain in the Caddo country after early April, and the ground dried and cracked. Only a few wild flowers came up, and even the weeds looked discouraged. Along the dry creek beds the trees began dropping their leaves in August.

Little Bear Woman and Mary worked at their beadwork; the little money it brought was all that the family had. But the women made as few trips to Colony as possible. The horses were poor and scrawny, and there was hardly enough prairie hay to feed them properly when they could find pasture at all, so the women tried not to use them.

Mr. Kincaide was very good. He gave them all the credit the Mohonk Conference, far away in New York State, would allow. But there was never a lack of water at Lake Mohonk, and the grasshoppers did not get that far. So the eastern people could not really understand what life was like in the Cheyenne country, or why the Indians needed as much money as they did.

At last, one Wednesday morning after breakfast, Jim said, "I guess we got to do something else. There's four of us, and little George eats more than his grandmother."

He had noticed that! Little Bear Woman always said she wasn't hungry and didn't want to eat, and she kept slipping food onto Mary's plate for the baby, but Mary had noticed how thin her mother was getting, and how easily she tired.

"We'll have to go somewhere else," Jim said. "I'll have to find a job somewhere."

"Maybe Colony?" Mary suggested. Whatever the problem was, she always thought of the Segers first.

"I'll ask Johnny," Jim agreed. He got up from the table and went out to the pasture. There he slipped the halter over the head of one horse. He rode away, and the two women waited all day, doing the routine things that must be done in a house, talking little, caring for the baby. Jim had not returned by sunset, and they ate some bread, drank some coffee made from toasted acorns, and still waited.

Mary had dozed into uneasy sleep when she heard Jim come into the bedroom. The moonlight was so bright she did not need to light the lamp to see him. His form and movements in the dimness were tired, but not discouraged.

"Where have you been?" she whispered.

"To Anadarko," Jim whispered back. He sat down on the edge of the bed and began to pull off his boots. "Johnny sent me. He gave me a note to the Agent. There was a teamster's job open and I got it. I start work Monday."

"That's only five days!" Mary protested. "Where are we going to live?"

"There's a house vacant at the Agency," Jim assured her. "Coffee had the job, but he quit. The house is going to need some fixing up. You know how Kiowas are. They don't take such good care of their houses."

"Johnny taught us a lot," Mary reflected. "What about Mother?" she asked.

"There's a room for her, and one next to ours for the baby," Jim reassured her. "It's a bigger house than this one. We'll be all right."

"Maybe we can try to rent this one next year if we decide to stay on," Mary said. She sighed a little. "I like it here, though."

"We can come back when we're ready," said Jim. "We don't have to stay away forever." But, as things turned out, they never went back.

After the flurry of moving and settling, Mary found she was pregnant again. During this pregnancy some of the old customs Little Bear Woman had insisted on had to be dropped. There was no place to build a little shelter for the delivery. Jim slept on the living room couch, but this time he grumbled a little, and sometimes he would sneak into the room, when Little Bear Woman was snoring, and sit beside Mary and they would talk. It was against all the Cheyenne rules, but they had very little time alone together, and they enjoyed those stolen moments.

This house had been painted all white inside, and Mary liked it, even if it did show dirt more than colors might. It reminded her of a tipi, and she told Jim so.

"We'll keep it that way, then," he decided, and when the Agent told them they could have paint from the Agency supply room, Jim brought home nothing but white.

There was no hospital at the Agency, but the Government had built one for Indians between Fort Sill and Lawton, a day's wagon drive to the south. A week before the baby was due, Jim took Mary there in the wagon.

Mary was sure she wouldn't like the hospital, or having a baby there. People had died in that hospital, she knew, and she had always been frightened by places of death.

"You'll be all right," Jim assured her. "This baby's half Caddo anyway, and Caddos aren't afraid of dead people. He'll be fine." He paused a moment. "I'd bring your mother down to be with you, but where would she stay?"

"No, you need her at home," said Mary. "You need someone to do your cooking and washing."

Much to her surprise, Mary found that she liked the hospital, and liked being there. It turned out she knew some of the women her own age who were there to have babies from the Colony, and she began to get acquainted with others. They all sat together on the high porch in front of the building and sewed or did beadwork, and talked endlessly about their babies and how they themselves felt.

"I'd like some dried meat," Bertha, a Comanche, remarked one day.

"Or some sweet corn," said Maude Campbell, who was a Kiowa and married to a Delaware.

"Wild plums would be good," Mary Pratt, an Arapaho, sighed.

"Oh, we've all been to school or we couldn't talk English to each other," Mary snapped. "The only thing I don't want is something stringy."

It almost seemed as if the cook had overheard them, for that night supper was macaroni and cheese. Mary took one look at it and pushed the tray away.

"Go on, eat it," the nurse told her. "It's good. It's good for you."

"You're trying to kill my baby," Mary said, and she began to cry. She felt the baby jump inside her, as if it, too, were trying to defend itself. "Take it away," Mary said. "The baby knows what he needs better than you do."

"You've got to eat something," the nurse protested, "and this is what the cook made."

"I'll eat plain bread," Mary announced, picking up a slice from the tray and biting into it.

"You're a stupid, stubborn Cheyenne," the nurse said, and she took away all the food except the one slice of bread in Mary's hand and left the room.

"They ought to have Indian nurses in these places, not white women," Mary said to Maude the next day. "What does she know about the right way to do things? An Indian nurse would have respect for the old ways."

Maude agreed with her. Without friends from the outside world to visit with, the hospital sometimes seemed a lonely, unfriendly place, in spite of the companionship the women shared. And the waiting was long and hard.

When Mary's time came, the nurse wheeled a stretcher to her bedside, and helped her to get on it and lie down. She was wheeled through the long white corridors, although she knew she was perfectly able to walk, and into a white room, with glass cabinets of glittering metal instruments and white lights overhead glaring down at her. Mary began to cry. She felt naked and alone; even more so when the nurse lifted her feet and put them high in stirrups at the end of the table on which they had laid her.

"That's all right," the nurse said, trying to reassure her. "It always hurts some, you know."

"I know," said Mary. She could not tell this strange woman that she was crying from homesickness, not pain. This was all wrong. Worst of all was the doctor, a man with a mustache. To have a man with her, now, seeing her like this! It was just all too much, and she struggled to free her feet from the stirrups and get down from the table. But the nurse put a wide canvas belt around her, and Mary stayed where she was.

The baby, another little boy, was born on August 28, 1902. She decided to call him Joe. He was fine and fat and healthy, but Mary was sure he would have a hard time all his life because of the way he had been born—not properly, in silence and seclusion, like an Indian baby, but under the glaring lights with white people looking on.

Afterward, she remembered other things about Joe's first days. They would not let her have him with her, not in her bed, not even in a crib in the same room. Instead, they took him away to what they called a "nursery," although they brought him back to his mother regularly to be fed. Mary even got used to being wakened in the middle of the night and the very early mornings, to take him. She asked the nurse why.

"Sometimes he's hungry and sometimes he isn't," Mary explained. "I have to pinch his bottom to keep him awake to nurse. Why do you do that to us?"

The nurse looked at her and shook her head.

"We have to keep him on a regular schedule," she said. "If you just let him eat when he feels like it, he'll grow up without any sense of time."

"That's the way Indians are," said Mary. "I never saw a clock until I went to school. My mother always had meat and fried bread for us, so we could eat when we wanted to. And my first baby was the same. I fed him when he got hungry and cried for it."

"It's all wrong," the nurse insisted, shaking her head. "The new one will be healthier when he grows up. You wait and see."

Mary stopped arguing. She could do what she liked with Joe when she took him home, and she told his father so when Jim came to see her on Sunday. Mary was sitting up in bed by then, but the hospital people wouldn't let her get on her feet.

"At home, I'd be doing the washing by now," she said to Jim.

"Could be they're right," Jim answered. "You get a good rest while you can. You'll have plenty of washing to do when you get home." He picked up a little box from the bedside table. "What's this?" he asked.

"It's his other half," Mary said. "They did do something part right," she continued. "They brought it to me, all right, but they brought me the whole thing. All I needed was a little piece to put in his beaded case. I don't know what to do with the rest of it!"

"Ask your mother when you get home," Jim suggested.

The first thing Mary said to her mother, when Jim took her home a week later, was, "What shall I do with this?" She showed Little Bear Woman the dried and shriveled navel cord.

Little Bear Woman laughed until she cried. "There's only one thing to do," she informed Mary. "Cut off what you need, and put it in his turtle case. Then we'll hang the rest on a white ash tree."

"There aren't any nearer than Colony," Mary reminded her.

"Then we'll go to Colony," Little Bear Woman declared.

It was another month before Jim could get a day off to drive them in the wagon to Colony. There, out of sight of the school, the church, and the employees' houses, they found a young white ash growing in a group of trees. Jim held the horses' heads and turned his own away while the two women tied the cord in the tree as high as Mary could reach.

"Let it grow with the tree and let him grow with both," prayed Little Bear Woman, stretching her arms to the sky. "Maheo, you know and love all growing things. Let this child grow, and let him live a long life."

"That's one thing that's been done right for this baby," Mary observed. It was good that her baby would have the protection of Maheo as well as of the white man's God, but she was still somewhat uneasy. Joe had not started out right, in the Indian way, and she feared life would always be hard for him.

Three more children—James, Maudie, and William—were born in the years that followed. All were born at the hospital, and Mary and Little Bear Woman made three more trips to the white ash tree at Colony.

Jim and Mary never moved back to the farm. Alice and her husband, Robert Cussen, rented it, because it adjoined Alice's, and Jim and Mary stayed on at the Agency.

11

LEARNING AGAIN

It was the following winter. Jim had been transferred to Riverside Indian School, where he was a boys' adviser. It was three miles away and on the other side of the Washita River, but they still lived in the house at the Agency. The Government people said they were going to build a row of new houses at the school for the employees, but so far there was no money to build more than a sort of clubhouse for the single employees and dormitories for the students. The married employees had to live at the Agency, or, if their houses were nearby, at home.

Mary didn't mind. She had got used to the house, and there was room for the children and her mother. Life went along steadily and quietly.

It was all so peaceful that Little Bear Woman said, "This would be a good time for you to begin to learn the things that only I can teach you. There are things you have a right to know, and someone in our family must carry them on. They belong to us, and you are the only one of my children near to me."

After that, they sat down on the living room floor together every day after noon dinner, and Little Bear Woman talked. Jim took his noon meal at school, so there was no one at home but the two women and the children, who were playing.

Little Bear Woman began at the beginning, when Maheo created the world. At first, there was nothing but darkness and water. She told how Maheo sent the ducks diving into the water for mud from which he would fashion the world, and how the ducks failed. At last Maheo was forced to send Turtle, who brought up mud from the bottom of the waters. With it, Maheo made rivers and mountains, and all living things, and finally he made men and women. The telling took a long time, because Mary had questions to ask and much to learn.

"It's like in Mr. Kincaide's Bible," Mary said wonderingly. "That says that the world was water and darkness at the beginning, and how God created the world the way we know it. It doesn't say anything about the turtle."

"Well, other people may believe differently from the Cheyennes," Little Bear Woman reminded her. "There are lots of other Cheyenne stories about turtles, but not all of them are sacred. The turtle carries the world and his house on his back. The most important animals, really, are the hawk and the buffalo."

The next day she began to tell the story of the Great Race between the animals, on one side, and men and the birds on the other: how a White Buffalo Woman appeared and raced the hawk, who beat her, and how ever after, men took all the things they needed for living from the buffalo—food, and clothing, and tipi covers, and all their utensils and their bowstrings and quivers and the sinew to bind on arrowheads. It was because of this that they reverenced the hawk and carried his feathers in their fans in the Sun Dance, and it was because of this, too, that there must always be a white buffalo skin tied to the center pole of the Sun Dance Lodge, in memory of the White Buffalo Woman.

These were all wonderful things, and Mary never forgot them. She tried to find a comparison with the Bible in the story of the Great Race, and she finally remembered the story of David and Goliath, and told that to her mother.

"You see," Little Bear Woman said, "religion is all the same. What you believe in your heart is what counts, not whether you call somebody David or Hawk."

Mary pondered this. "There aren't any Cheyenne giants," she reminded her mother.

"Oh, yes, there are," Little Bear Woman said. "Wait here."

She went to her own room, and brought back the bundle that had always hung above her brother's bed and now hung above hers.

"I am an old woman, and I want you to have this," she said. She laid the bundle on the floor between them, with the knots of the tie strings up. Three times she reached to untie each knot, and the fourth time she unfastened one of the four ties. She laid the bundle open, and for the first time Mary saw what was in it.

There was a fan, made of a whole hawk's wing. There were little buckskin bags of paints, so old the colors had stained through the hide. There was a tiny bowl, made from the burl of a tree Mary didn't know.

"It's maple," Little Bear Woman said. "That tree grows far to the north, and it is always warm. Hold it in your hand, and see for yourself."

Mary picked up the bowl and held it. Truly, she felt warmth spreading through her hand and up her arm. "What is it good for?" she asked.

"It is to mix medicines," said Little Bear Woman. She showed Mary buckskin bags of herbs, and a great swatch of sweet grass tied in a bundle. She took an old, black stone, shaped like a piece of backbone, and showed it to Mary, with a small horn spoon. "When someone is ill, you hold the stone over him and move it around from one part of his body to the other. When it gets heavy and hot in your hand, you will know where the sickness is. Then keep looking at the stone until you can see through it, and you will know what the sickness is. Brush the sickness all together in one place with the hawk-feather fan, and put this"—she held out the tip of a buffalo horn—"over it, to draw the sickness out. Suck it out with your mouth and spit it into the fire. Then mix your medicines in the bowl with the spoon and paint the place so you won't forget where you brushed the sickness together—red for a man and yellow for a woman. Pour in clean water, and give it to the sick one to drink. If you believe, he will get well."

Mary considered. "It's hard," she ventured at last.

"All learning is hard," her mother reminded her. "This is only the beginning of this kind of learning. There are songs to go with every motion, and you must learn them, too. And remember"—her voice was very stern—"if you do not do this with love and pity in your heart; if you have one evil or unkind thought while you are doing it, the patient will die and someone you love will die, too. It must all be done with love and pity, not just in your mouth, but in your heart."

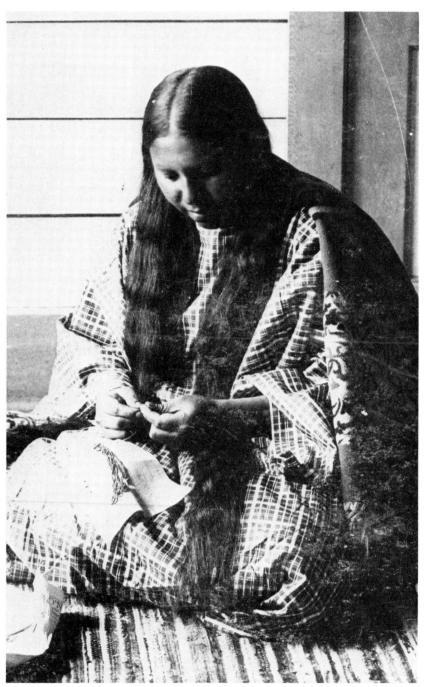

Mary's mother, Little Bear Woman, beading moccasins at Mohonk Lodge, Seger Colony.

Mary Inkanish, left, at about age fifteen; the other girl is either her sister or a friend.

James D. Inkanish, Mary's
husband.

Mary Long Hand Inkanish,
Caddo; Jim's mother.

James Inkanish, left, and Robert Cross.

Caddo dress.

Mary, standing, fourth from left, at Anadarko. White woman, sitting at left, is Susie Peters, the Field Woman who taught Mary to drive a car.

The Women's Heart Club on tour in Gallup, New Mexico. Mary is in the bottom row, center; her daughter Josephine is in the top row, at far left.

Joseph Inkanish, son of Mary and James.

Josephine, with dolls, at about three years.

Josephine, in Cheyenne clothes, about the time she was elected Cheyenne Princess.

Josephine, closeup, with Cheyenne dress and jewelry.

A Caddo powwow. Josephine is second from left; on her left is Alice Cussen, her aunt.

Josephine, right, and her Kiowa friend, Augustine Campbell.

Alice Cussen—Jim's sister, Mary's sister-in-law.

Mary and Jim at the San Francisco Indian Exposition, 1939. They are wearing Caddo clothes.

Mary was awed. "I don't think I can do it," she said at last. "I don't think I am strong enough. Only a person who is very good and strong, like you, can do it."

"There was a time when you did not think I was good," Little Bear Woman reminded her. "You thought I was wicked, and you said so, to my face."

Tears streamed down Mary's face, and her body shook with sobs. "That's what I mean," she wept. "If I could do that to you—my own mother—I have no right to be the guardian of sacred things."

"They aren't sacred to you," Little Bear Woman said. "These things are sacred to the Cheyennes, and you're a Christian."

Mary cried more bitterly. "I don't know what I am," she said. "Sometimes I'm one thing and sometimes another. Sometimes I think I'm Indian and other times I know I'm white."

Little Bear Woman put her arms around her daughter, and rocked her gently back and forth, like a child. "You'll find out someday," she comforted Mary. "When the time comes, you'll know. Until then, it won't do you any harm to know something about each kind of life."

"How will I know?" Mary asked. She honestly wanted to find out if there was a way of recognizing herself.

"You will know," Little Bear Woman insisted. "No one can tell you how or when, but when the time comes, you will know." She shook Mary gently. "Look in the bundle again. There is something I want you to have now."

Hesitantly, Mary reached out her hand. Hardly realizing what she was doing, she made four attempts before she finally touched it. Then she laid back the cover and disclosed, lying among the bags of herbs, a necklace of bone beads. Why hadn't she seen it before? she wondered. The beads were very old, four short strands made to tie close around the neck. From the front hung a pendant, a single shell, fastened to the necklace by a strand of very old glass beads.

Mary had never seen anything like it before. All the bone necklaces she had seen were made of big bone tubes, strung vertically. This was different. The beads were tiny, and were strung horizontally.

"It is yours," Little Bear Woman said, lifting it on the fourth gesture toward her. "It was mine when I was a young woman, and now it is yours. You can give it to your daughter when she is old enough to show what Cheyenne family she belongs to. The shell is round, like a turtle's shell, and it means you are one of the turtle people."

"With the whole world on my back?" Mary laughed shakily.

"With the whole world on your back," her mother repeated. "You'll know the weight of it soon enough. You felt some of it already, when your uncle died."

Later that night, when they were in bed alone and the house was quiet, Mary told Jim about the bundle. "I don't think I ought to take it," she finished. "It doesn't seem right, somehow. Something bad might happen."

"Nothing bad will happen when I am here," Jim said, and drew her close.

But Mary was still uneasy. She waited four weeks, while her mother continued teaching her. Then they went to Colony in the wagon, and while her mother was peering over the beads and choosing colors for a pair of moccasins for Joe, Mary left her and went to see Minnie.

"She wants me to take that bundle that was her brother's," she said in Cheyenne. No need to explain anything more to Minnie.

"Don't you want it?" Minnie asked.

"I'm afraid. Something bad might happen," Mary reiterated.

Minnie sat still, with her head bent. "I know people said when I changed my name that something bad would happen to me," she said. "Well, it has. I'll never have any children of my own, the doctors say."

Mary sat still, stunned. "How do they know?" she burst out at last. "How can you be sure? They haven't any right to tell you something like that."

Minnie shook her head, resignedly. "You don't know," she said. "When you say something bad will happen to a person, then it can. Don't say it about yourself. You might put a curse on you."

"I'll give you one of my boys," Mary offered impulsively.

Again Minnie shook her head. "That won't make things any different. It will still be one of your boys, and everyone will know it. No, Vee-hay-kah. I love you and I love your children, but I won't take one from you—not now. That might make things worse."

"The Reverend Givvens used to say we make our own fates, with the help of the Lord," Mary mused. "I don't think we ought to make our children's fates, too. Is that what you mean?"

"That, but parents do make their children's fates," said Minnie. She got up briskly. "Now I make us coffee," she said in English, and Mary knew that Minnie would talk no more about the matter.

Again she confided in Jim in the night-quiet of the house. "I feel so bad for Minnie, poor thing," she ended, "and I know she thinks I'm to blame."

"You're not to blame," Jim said reasonably. He was always sensible. "And you know, she's just been talking to white doctors. Why doesn't she try that peyote the Comanches and Kiowas have. They say it's powerful. It works when other medicines won't."

"I don't know if she believes in Indian doctoring or not," Mary said. Minnie probably did, though. If she believed in Indian curses, she probably believed in Indian cures.

"I'll talk to Robert," Jim repeated. "It's worth trying, anyway."

He fell asleep then, and Mary felt safer because Jim *would* talk to Robert if he said he would.

When they had all talked around and around about it, Minnie herself settled the matter. "We make our own fates, as Mary says," she reminded them. "I have to live with this."

Most of all, Mary wondered about her necklace. It had come out of the bundle, but it had been her mother's, and she prized it for that. But she could not bring herself to wear it. She excused putting it away in the drawer under her scarf by saying it did not go with her white woman's clothes, and was too precious to wear around the house with her reservation dresses. It was, in a way, a part of the Indian-white puzzle she was more and more aware of as she tried to solve it.

Now and again, Mary thought that perhaps if she went back to school she might find a solution. If she studied hard to become a teacher, she might at the same time become all white. But there were Jim and the children to think of. And her mother. No. She could not leave any one of them, let alone all. She shook her head at her own foolishness, and went back to being an Indian housewife living within a white man's walls.

Four walls to each room; four straight, square walls. She swept them as religiously as she swept the floors. In a tipi the walls would have gradually deepened in color from the cooking smoke, but these walls were rigid, and the same unrelenting shade of government white. She asked Jim to see if she might repaint them herself, using some of the money she was accumulating from the beadwork she did for Mr. Kincaide, but the Agent refused. White paint was what the government had issued for those walls, and white they should remain. No fancy colors in *his* Agency.

Minnie came from Colony to spend a few days, and she made a suggestion. Like Mary, Minnie had white walls and had to keep them white, but she had found a way to add some color to her house.

"Get some window curtains to go over those old yellow shades," Minnie said. "Put the curtains on the inside of the room, so the shades show from the outside, and nobody will know the difference."

Together, they walked into town that afternoon, and at the dry goods store they looked at every piece—every bolt—of calico.

"I want different curtains for each room," Mary said, by way of explanation for her thoroughness.

It was not easy to find four bolts of colors that they both liked. At last the two women decided on turquoise for the living room, a bright yellow printed with forget-me-nots for the kitchen, a soft green for Little Bear Woman's room, and for the bedrooms, pink—a bright pink, not a washed-out one.

"When they get dirty, you can take them down and wash them," Minnie said. "And if you want to, you can change them around from one room to the other."

"I used to like white because it reminded me of a tipi but now I'm tired of it. When I have my own house, I'll make the walls any color I want them," said Mary. "A different color for every room. And I'll have real curtains, from the store, not just homemade ones."

A house! A house of her own!

Some of the white employees at the Agency had bought houses in town, and lived there. Why shouldn't Jim and Mary be able to do the same thing?

"We had our own house on the allotment," she reminded him, when they talked it over.

"Yes, but we *had* the house," Jim replied. "Maybe Indians can't buy houses in town."

"I'm going to find out," Mary informed him, and she did.

Two or three days later she saw the Agent, Mr. Bunton, walking across the open, parklike space around which the employees' houses were set. The Agency was laid out that way because that was the way Army posts were laid out, and the plans for them already were on hand in Washington. That anyone would find the open, tree-shaded area that took the place of the Army parade ground pleasant for picnics, and even concerts from the Riverside Indian School band, was hardly a consideration in the planning. But the area was there, and eventually it became known as the "recreation area."

Mary often thought that if Mr. Bunton had been a woman, he would have been a fine housekeeper. When he walked—and he walked a lot—he inspected every blade of grass and every leaf that fell from every tree. He stopped in front of Mary's house to examine a sycamore and make sure its bark was peeling correctly, and Mary went out on the porch and spoke to him. "Good evening," she said softly.

Mr. Bunton jerked around, and looked up at her. Employees and their families seldom interrupted his walks, "Good evening, Mary," he returned. "How are you?"

"I'm fine, Mr. Bunton. How are you?"

"Oh, very well, Mary. Very well. This tree looks well, too." He smiled at her, a small, plump woman in her plum-colored reservation dress. "Can I do something for you," he asked.

"Mr. Bunton, will you answer me one question," she asked. Her hands twisted together nervously.

"If I can," the Agent replied.

"Mr. Bunton, is there any Government rule that Indians can't buy houses in town?"

Mr. Bunton considered, for what seemed to Mary like a long

time. He was like one of the older men, in council, she thought. "Do you want a house in town?" he asked at last. "Don't you like it, living here at the Agency?"

"I like it, I guess," said Mary. She considered things, in her turn. "I got friends here, and all. We get along all right. But I was thinking. Maybe I'll have another baby. Maybe it could be a girl. It would be nice for her to have her own house when she grows up."

Mr. Bunton, who had worked with Indians all his grown-up life and been in many places, laughed. "You talk like a New Mexico Pueblo woman," he joked. "They all want their own houses."

"Every woman wants her own house," Mary assured him seriously. "Pueblo or Cheyenne makes no difference. A Pueblo woman wants one of them mud houses you talk about, and a Cheyenne woman wants her own tipi. Either way, she can pass it down to her daughter."

"I see," Mr. Bunton said. "That's a reason, certainly. And no, Mary, I don't know of any Government rules or state laws that say Indians can't have their own houses, if they want them and can pay for them. Why don't you and Jim go to the courthouse, and talk to the county clerk? He might give you good advice—even know about a house you could buy and pay for a little at a time."

"Thank you," Mary said. She started into the house, and then turned back suddenly. "Mr. Bunton, if something happened so we couldn't pay for that house, could anybody take it away from us?"

"Not if you honestly told them what happened, and perhaps paid a little less every month for a while," Mr. Bunton said. "I don't think you and Jim would have any trouble, Mary. You both work hard and most people respect you and think a lot of you. Some Indians—people who drink, or stay up all night at peyote meetings—might have trouble, but you and Jim shouldn't. Try it and see. You won't know if you don't try. You're part white, too. That makes a difference."

It was a startlingly new thought. This was an advantage of being part white Mary had never thought of. It didn't make things easier in the Indian world, she knew. She and Jim were shut out of ceremonies and dances they might have liked to go to because of her white blood. Now it seemed to Mary that there were advantages in being part white.

On Friday afternoon Jim took a half-day off, and they went into Anadarko and to the courthouse. The red brick building, with a tower rising two stories above the two that made up the rest of the structure, looked imposing. They were a little awed by the size of the place, but Jim took Mary's hand in his, under her shawl, and they went up the white limestone steps worn by the feet that had gone that way before them, and into the wooden-floored hall. Its walls were stained from hands pressing against them, and the heads that had leaned back against them as people sat on the backless benches paralleling each side. The floor was stained and greasy from floor-sweep. Down at the other end of the hall, facing them, a gilt sign projected. "County Clerk" it read, and Mary and Jim walked toward it.

The door beneath the sign stood open into the office, where a counter, shoulder-high on Mary, separated the clerk and his helpers from visitors. It was like the Agent's office used to be, thought Mary, before Mr. Bunton came, and made the workmen put in a low railing. Whatever became of that counter, Mary wondered, and turned her attention back to the office, and the man who faced her.

"What do you want?" the man asked in a hoarse rancher's voice. You could tell he didn't think much of Indians, or know much about them, by the way he spoke.

"We want to buy a house," Jim said quietly. "Mr. Bunton told us you might know about a house in town we could buy."

"Buy a house!" the clerk yelled. He turned to two or three men behind him at the desks. "Hey, you fellows, listen to this. Here's a couple Indians wants to buy a house!"

The other men guffawed. Mary hung her head, and clutched Jim's arm more firmly against her side.

"Why not?" Jim asked. "I'm a Government employee, and we live in a house at the Agency. We want one of our own."

"They want a house!" the clerk reiterated. "I bet you already got a house of your own, paid for out of us taxpayers' pockets, too."

"Yes, we have a house," Jim said, as quietly as before. "It's on an allotment at Binger. But I got a job, too, and it's at Riverside Indian School. I can't go back and forth every day. It takes half a day each way. I got no time to work if I do that."

"Then stay home and work your allotment," the clerk snapped.

"Live in that house the Government built and we paid for. Your squaw will do all the farming anyway."

Suddenly Mary's head went up. She came out of her shawl like a turtle out of its shell, and she glared at the white man before her as if she would put his eyes out with the hate in hers.

"You make me sick!" she hissed. "You all time talking 'bout lazy Indians and squaws and things you don't know nothin' about"—she knew her English was getting worse and worse, and she didn't care—"but when one of us, just one, tries to get ahead and do what you say he ought to do, you push him back, and you call his wife dirty names." Her chin quivered, and she bit her tongue till she stopped shaking. "You're the ones who make lazy Indians and don't care what they do."

"Hey, look here," the clerk began. "I never said you couldn't have a house. You can buy one just like anybody else if you got money and references. Get out of here and over to the bank, and tell them what you just told me." A sort of grudging respect came into his voice. "I never knew a squ—an Indian like you. Go on. Talk to them at the bank, and see what happens."

Mary's head was still high as she marched through the door, the way she'd been taught to march at Colony, step for step with Jim. They crossed the street in front of the courthouse and walked down a side street to the bank.

Here there was another of those forbiddingly high counters. On the other side was a young woman, and she smiled at Mary and avoided staring at either of them.

"What can I do for you?" she asked.

All the fight went out of Mary. Kindness disarmed her as rudeness never could. "We want to buy a house," she almost whispered. Jim had drawn into himself before this strange woman, and left the talking to Mary.

"That's a good idea," said the woman. She flashed a gold tooth at them in a quick smile. "What kind of a house do you want? A farmhouse?"

"We have a farmhouse," Jim took over. "We want a house in town. I work at Riverside, and we got some children. I don't want them to go to Indian school like we had to. I want them to go to public school."

"Well!" said the young woman. "Well! I never heard anything like that before. It will cost you money to send them to public school, you know. You'll have to buy their clothes and books. Besides paying for the house," she added, almost as an afterthought.

"We can do it," Jim said. "I've got a job, and my wife's a good beadworker. We can both work and earn money. We'll get along. We already pay rent to the Agency for the house we live in there. It comes out of my salary. Better we pay rent to ourselves, and own the house we live in when we're done."

"You're right!" the woman said. She flashed her tooth again. "I'm part Cherokee myself, and I'm always urging our full-bloods to go to work and get ahead."

"I'm full-blood," Jim declared proudly. "But my wife here, she's half white." He took Mary's hand and gave it a reassuring squeeze, under the shawl. "We can make out."

"Come on in," said the Cherokee woman, and she opened a door in the counter. They passed through to the other side, and in that one step their whole lives changed, without their knowing it.

12

JOSEPHINE

The house they finally found and bought seemed to Mary the finest place she had ever seen. It had a big living room, with a bedroom opening off one side. At the other end of the living room was the dining room, with the kitchen behind it. Opening off the dining room, paralleling it and the kitchen, was a hall, with two more bedrooms and a bathroom. And there was a closet in each bedroom, and a door opened from the front bedroom into the hall.

Josephine was born at home, on June 3, 1917, when Mary was forty and the other children were growing up. She refused to bear this last child, who she hoped and prayed would be another girl, in the Indian hospital.

They could not do everything in the old way now that they were living in town, of course. Two weeks before the baby was due, Jim and the boys moved to a dormitory room at Riverside School.

"I wouldn't do this for anybody but you and Mary," the Superintendent told Jim with a grin. "But if she wants to be old-fashioned, up to a point, I'll help you out."

"Thanks," Jim said. He grinned, too. "It's her mother, really, I guess. That old lady would have us all living in tipis yet, I believe, if she could get her way. She says she won't learn English for anybody, but she sure gave the boys a bawling-out the other day for playing with the baby's things. She's made over that old cradle Minnie made for George and fixed it up real pretty with a new blue calico lining, and the boys were trying to carry it when she caught them. They don't speak anything but English, and she sure told them how the cow ate the cabbage without speaking any Cheyenne."

Josephine was a pretty, plump, brown little thing.

"She looks like you, when you were tiny," Little Bear Woman said. "Her eyes are even gray-blue."

Mary, resting in the big brass bed Jim had bought for this occasion, smiled. "I don't care what color her eyes are," she said. "She's my daughter, that's all I care about. I love her."

It seemed as if Josephine had come into the world to love and be loved by everyone. She never cried. When she needed changing, she pouted her lips at her mother, but that was the only expression of displeasure she had. Usually she was smiling, and she learned to laugh out loud when she was a month old, before most babies do. She never crawled, but at nine months she started walking. Little Bear Woman thought this was too soon for any child to walk, that she should be kept in her cradle till she was a year and a half old. Mary was firm, however. She would put Josephine in the cradle to sleep, but placed the cradle itself in a child's bed with sides that slid up and down. And she never tied Josephine to the backboard.

"She's the only child in town who has two beds," Jim laughed, but he let Mary have her way about it.

Mary took Josephine to Sunday School at the Presbyterian church from the time she was two. Everyone else said it was too soon, that Josephine wouldn't understand anything, but whether she understood or not, she was quiet and good, and she loved to sing hymns. "Jesus loves me, this I know," she peeped one morning, and Mary swept her up in her arms and hugged her.

"Everybody loves you," she said. "Why should Jesus be different?" Then she stopped and thought. "Who was Jesus?" she asked Josephine.

"I don't know," Josephine said, smiling as always. "Some man, I guess. Anyway, He loves me, 'cause the Bible tells me so." There was nothing to answer. If Josephine understood that much, a thousand years of teaching wouldn't teach her any more.

Josephine was not only good, she was a healthy little girl. She drank her milk— How many times did Mary think of Johnny Seger when she filled the child's glass?—and she minded her parents. When she started school, she brought home about the same medium grades as her brothers and sister had, but she always had A's in Conduct and Deportment.

And from the time Josephine was thirteen years old she knew what she wanted to be—a teacher. "Don't you want to get married and have babies of your own?" Mary asked her one day.

"After a while, I guess," Josephine replied. "I want to be a teacher first, though. Then I can teach my own children."

"There isn't any end to teaching and learning," Mary said, smoothing the child's hair. "Those things go on as long as you live."

"Can I go to college, too?" Josephine asked. "They say that's where you learn most, in college."

"We'll see," was all that Mary said, but from that time on she put away every penny she made from beadwork, and all that her mother gave her, so Josephine could go to college.

The early 1930's brought strange, hard times for many Indians. Heat and drought invaded their lands. The Dust Bowl days brought much suffering, and the depression throughout the country was felt in their world. The old days and the old ways were gone; it was as if Johnny and the teachers and the preachers had driven them away. The old people, too, were going fast. Almost nobody spoke of the Sun Dance anymore; when they did, it was as if they spoke of some long-ago secret.

There were times when the people who had not learned how to farm or work at white man's jobs often went hungry. At such times they came to Mary and Jim, or to others who had learned to work, and those who had money and food shared with those who had not. But whatever happened, even if she went without a meal or two herself, Mary kept her little bit of money put away for Josephine's education. Never would she touch that, no matter how great their needs.

Minnie gave Josephine her Cheyenne name. It was the summer the girl was thirteen, and there was a big powwow at about the same time they would have held the Sun Dance in the old days. Minnie, her awl concealed in her hand, led Josephine into the center of the dance ring during the afternoon give-aways. She spoke to the camp caller, and told him what to say, in a whisper.

"Listen to me, all you people," the man said when Minnie had given him his instructions. "This young girl's mother and the woman with her have been friends since they were little girls, younger than this one. Now Minnie wants to give her friend's daughter a Cheyenne name. Speak up, Minnie. Tell them how they are to know this girl."

"I name her Mah-hee-yuna," Minnie said, and with flashing quickness she pierced Josephine's earlobes with her awl and thrust little gold wires through them. She twisted the wires into loops. "She shall be an honored child, to her own family and to all the Cheyenne people," Minnie said. "In her honor I wish to give away four blankets."

The announcer called the names of the four women who were to receive the blankets. They were all members of the Sewing Women's Society, and friends of Little Bear Woman. The people called out in praise of Minnie and Josephine and their families.

"Why did you name her that?" Mary asked Minnie afterward. They were alone in camp. Jim was smoking with Robert in Minnie's camp; the boys were out playing baseball with their friends; and Josephine had gone to show off her new gold earrings to some northern Cheyennes who had come for the celebration. "That's my mother's name. Why did you give her the name of a living person?"

"It's not really a name," Minnie answered slowly. "It's more of a title. And you know what it means—the woman who gives herself for all the people. I wanted it to be kept alive, so people will never forget how important Cheyenne women are."

"But my mother is still living," Mary protested again. "You can't give one living person another's name."

"I did," Minnie said, defiantly. And that was the end of the matter, as far as she was concerned.

Little Bear Woman left them the following winter. Usually, she was up and about even before Mary, and when Mary did not find her mother in the kitchen—when she waked with no smell of coffee in the house—she went to Little Bear Woman's room to see what was wrong. Little Bear Woman lay quietly in her bed, her eyes closed, her mouth turned in a little smile, and the bundle hung over her head. At first Mary thought her mother was asleep, but when she touched Little Bear Woman's forehead to waken her, it was cold.

"Jim! Jim!" Mary cried, and he and the boys came running to

her. A moment later Josephine came, in her long wrapper, waves of black hair pouring over her shoulders. Jim took his daughter's arm and turned her away.

"Go and get dressed," he said, "and then go to the Agency and have them send word for Minnie. Your mother will need her."

It was a moment and forever before Minnie was there. The Agency telephone was working that day, and so was the one at Mohonk Lodge, so sending for Minnie was quicker than in the old days when they would have had to put a boy on a horse to go.

"Thank you for coming," Mary said, and she put her arms around her friend and they wept together. Together they dried their eyes, and went back to the bedroom. They took away the bedding to be burned; they bathed Little Bear Woman and perfumed her body with sage and sweet grass, combed her hair, and painted her face, all for the last time. Little Bear Woman had made her own burial moccasins long before. The two younger women put her thin little feet—almost like a child's feet—in them, and slipped a gray dress over her head. Little Bear Woman had given her buckskin dress and German silver jewelry to Josephine long before. Minnie brought an embroidered shawl, and Mary took her own silver earrings from her ears and fastened them into her mother's.

Minnie took up the medicine bundle.

"She will want this, too," she said, but Mary contradicted her. "She gave it to me and told me how to care for it before Josephine was born. I'll keep it. I'm the only one left."

"Do you think you ought to?" Minnie asked. "It belonged to the dead—to many who are dead. You told me once that something bad would happen if you took it."

"I remember that I was afraid something bad would happen, but it will be all right," Mary replied, without explaining more. She picked up the bundle. "I'll put it away in the suitcase. Nobody will see it or handle it."

The hearse, painted black and drawn by two black horses, came then. Jim and Robert and the boys picked up the tiny blanket-wrapped bundle that had been Little Bear Woman, and laid it in the hearse.

"Old-time funeral, I see," said the driver, and Jim replied "Yes," and got into the buggy with Mary and Josephine.

The cemetery was on the hillside west of town, sloping to the west. It was one of those deceptively warm, sunny afternoons that sometimes comes in the middle of winter. They laid Little Bear Woman in the opened earth, and Mary put a little enamelware bucket of food and coffee at her feet, for the journey she was to take. Jim stood with his hat off, and his face turned to the sky.

"God," he said, "you know this was a good woman. Whatever she did, she did because she believed in the Above Person, and I guess He was You. She called him another name, but that doesn't make any difference. Take her home to You."

People had gathered at the house by the time they got back, leaving the newly filled grave as a scar on the earth behind them. Some of the people from the Agency and the school had brought food, and they all ate together.

When the meal was over, Mary stood up. "You all knew my mother," she began. She choked a little, then went on, when her voice steadied. "She was an old-time Cheyenne woman. She followed the old-time ways. She didn't have much, but what she had, I want to give away to her friends. She believed in that custom. First I am going to cut my hair, because I mourn for her. But I shan't cut my finger or shed any blood, because she wouldn't let me do that when her brother died."

Mary picked up her sewing shears, and cut her hair as close to her head as she could. It fell to the floor, and lay around her feet, while she gave away her mother's tanning tools, her awl, a bundle of sinew, and hanks of beads to the Sewing Women who were present. When it was all done, Mary walked out of the room and into her bedroom, and lay down on the bed.

Josephine followed her. "Now you will have to teach me," Josephine said.

"I want you to be taught in college," Mary said. "The old Cheyennes are dying, and their ways with them. Let them go. You will live in another world."

"They'll never die while you're alive," Josephine said, and ran her hand over her mother's short hair. "I love you. I don't want your ways to die."

Mary sat up. "Life belongs to the living," she reminded her daughter. "You are young and alive. Forget all this, and be happy in the world you live in."

Minnie came in then. "Go on, now," she said to Josephine. "Let your mother rest a while. I'll sit with her."

They were very quiet when Josephine left the room. Mary lay on the bed, and Minnie sat beside her.

At last Minnie said, "She wants to be a Cheyenne."

"She isn't," Mary said flatly. "I'm half white, and you know it. Her father's a Caddo, and they live more like white people than Indians. She wants to go to college; she wants to be a teacher. That means she'll have to live like a white woman."

By spring Josephine was a pretty thing, and the boys began to notice her. One of them asked her to go to a school dance with him.

"May I, Mother?" Josephine asked. "May I go?"

"Do you like him?" Mary asked, "or do you just want people to notice you?"

"I like him," Josephine answered. "I like him better than any of the other boys."

"Then you can go," Mary decided, "but you'll have to go like a Cheyenne."

"You mean wear my buckskin dress to a *school party?*" Josephine demanded. She thought about it. "It might be nice, I guess," she decided. "Nobody else would have one."

"Not your buckskin dress," Mary laughed. "I'll get you a new dress at Levy's. But you'll go like a Cheyenne. You'll see."

The dress was wine-red silk crepe and very becoming. On the evening of the school dance, before Josephine put her dress on, Mary walked into the girl's room with her sewing kit.

"Pull up your slip," she ordered. When Josephine obeyed, Mary sewed her firmly into her panties, and put an added strip of muslin around her waist and between her legs. "Now any boy will have to respect you," she declared. "My mother did this for me when I was growing up. I'm not going to take any chances. I don't want you hurt."

"What if I have to go to the rest room?" Josephine wailed.

"You won't," Mary informed her sternly.

When Josephine came home that night, Mary was waiting up for her. "Did you manage?" she inquired.

A look of surprise crossed Josephine's face. "I didn't have to go!" she exclaimed. "But I do now," she added, and ran down the hall to the bathroom, Mary and the scissors in quick pursuit.

In the summer of 1933 the Caddos decided to elect a Princess. They had heard that some of the northern tribes, like the Sioux and Crows, had Princesses, and the tribal council thought that they should have one, too. They set up ballot boxes—usually shoe boxes with the lids glued on and slits cut in the tops so ballots could be inserted—in stores around Anadarko. Any Caddo who bought a dollar's worth of goods could vote, and he could vote once for each dollar he spent. Some of the Wichitas and Delawares voted, too. They claimed that the Wichitas were related to the Caddos, and that an Indian Princess was an Indian Princess, and the other, smaller tribes should have some say in the choice. The Kiowas and Comanches were jealous because they hadn't thought of the idea first, but they pulled themselves together and each tribe elected its own Princess. The merchants helped them, too. It was all good for business.

The boxes were opened on a Saturday afternoon, when most of the Indians were in town. The other storekeepers brought their boxes to Jake Tingley's pawnshop, on Broadway, the "Indian Main Street" of the town. Everyone liked Jake and everyone trusted him, so it had been agreed that he should open the boxes and he and his brother should count the votes.

Jake and his brother stood behind the counter, with the store packed with Caddos, Wichitas, and Delawares, while Kiowas, Comanches, and Apaches thronged the sidewalk and spilled over into the street. Mary and Jim had been the first to get there, as soon as Jake opened up in the morning, and Minnie and Robert were right behind them. Of course, they hoped Josephine would win; at the same time they hardly dared think about it. Josephine herself wouldn't come. She was too nervous. She did slip down to the back door and pass a bag of sandwiches through to Jake's daughter, Irma. Nobody could get out of the store by then. Josephine had made enough sandwiches for Irma and Jake and his brother, as well as Robert and Minnie and her parents, so they all had enough to eat, and they blessed Josephine for her thoughtfulness.

By this time, Mary was nervous, too—too nervous to eat. She

tried, and Minnie and Irma coaxed her, but all she could get down was a bottle of pink pop Irma took out of her father's cooler. Jake always kept pink pop on hand for his Indian customers. Mary wanted to pay for the pop, but Irma wouldn't let her.

"The sandwiches are worth more than a bottle of pop," she said, and that ended it.

By three o'clock everyone, inside the store and out, was excited and nervous. Then they saw the United States Marshal riding down the street from the post office. Behind him came the other shopkeepers with their boxes. They all pushed through the crowd, and the Marshal sat his horse in front of the door while the businessmen made their way inside. They put the boxes on the counter in front of Jake and his brother.

Very carefully, using the small blades of their pocket knives, the two men cut open the glued-on lids of the boxes and took out the folded ballots. The girls' names were written on all kinds of paper: sales slips, torn-off corners of newspapers, scraps of brown paper bags, and even some on the fancy pink paper Mrs. Levy used when she wrapped wedding and baby presents. Jake and his brother divided the slips into piles, by the girls' names. Then, deliberately, slowly, they counted each pile and wrote down the number of votes it showed.

Mary was sure afterward that she held her breath from the time the Marshal pulled his horse across the doorway until Jake finally looked up from the bill of sale he was using as a tally sheet.

"Josephine Inkanish wins," he announced. "She has three hundred and ninety-eight votes. Next closest is Martha Beaver, with one hundred and thirty-five. You sure got a lot of good friends, Jim."

Some people cheered, and some people grumbled, and everyone began to move away.

Minnie put her arms around Mary. "You'll always be proud of her, and remember this day," she whispered. Like Mary, Minnie was crying with joy and relief.

Now they had to decide about Josephine's dress. There was going to be a parade down Main Street and up Broadway on the morning of the Fourth of July, and a big picnic at the Agency park, and then the tribal Princesses would be crowned.

Josephine wanted to wear her grandmother's buckskin dress,

but Mary put her foot down. "If you were a Cheyenne princess it would be all right," she declared, "but if you're a Caddo princess, you'll have to dress like a Caddo."

They got out all the old photographs they could find, and pored over them. One of them, taken by an Army officer years ago, showed a group of Wichita girls with their long hair falling over their bare breasts, and sullen faces. Josephine giggled when she saw it. "I could dress like that," she said. "It wouldn't use up much material, just an old blanket. I wonder who these girls are." She turned the picture over. "Some of the women are beauties" was written on the back in old-fashioned slanting script.

Cheyenne modesty prevailed. Mary made a skirt of rose color, with a wide ruffle of deeper rose around the bottom. The blouse was so pale it was almost white. Jim's sister Alice made the apron, as long as the skirt, of stiff white organdy, the waistband tied in a full bow at the back. It was lovely, but Mary fussed. "It's too plain," she said; "it needs some jewelry." But the old bone necklace was Cheyenne. She tried it around Josephine's neck, but it just didn't look right.

Then, on the first of July, Jim's old aunt appeared at the door. They seldom saw her anymore. She lived in Binger, and almost never left her allotment.

"Hello," said Mary, opening the screen. "Come in. How did you get here?"

"My neighbors brought me," Jim's aunt said, stepping into the living room.

"Come and drink coffee," Mary offered. "You must be tired."

"I am," replied the aunt, "but I wanted to come. I want to see Jim's girl made a Princess." She followed Mary into the kitchen, and they sat at the table, drinking coffee and eating some little sweet store-cakes Jim had bought the day before. The old aunt placed a shawl-wrapped bundle on the floor beside her.

"You have a nice house," she observed, looking around her.

"I have a good husband," Mary reminded her.

Jim came in then, and Mary got up with a start. Dinnertime! Then she looked at the clock. Jim was early; it was only eleven, after all, not twelve-fifteen, his usual time.

"I heard you were here," Jim said politely.

"I brought something," she answered, and picked up her package. She laid the shawl open on the kitchen table. It was not like any Mary had ever seen before; a dark brown background, with an all-over red and blue pattern on it. "It came from far away," Jim's aunt said. "It was my mother's, and she brought it with her when the Caddos were moved from Texas. She brought these other things, too."

Inside the shawl, lying against the sheer wool, she laid out strings and strings of tiny, shiny black beads, tied together with a bow of worn and faded plaid ribbon. "It will need a new tie," she said, fingering it. She laid back the last corner of the shawl.

Inside the last corner of the shawl was another piece of jewelry. It was flat, and shaped like the hourglasses Mary remembered in pictures in her old readers. About the span of a woman's spread fingers, it was stiff rawhide, which showed in a few places through the thin black silk cloth that covered it. The cloth was held in place with small silver buttons, set closely all over it, and there were more of the old plaid silk ribbons hanging from the underside.

"What is it?" Mary asked curiously. "I never saw anything like it before."

"It's old, old," Jim's aunt told her. "It belonged to my grandmother. Caddo women wore them on the backs of their heads when they dressed up for dancing. Delaware women used to wear them, too. Maybe the Caddos got the idea from them. I don't know. But this was my grandmother's, and now I want Jim's girl to have it, and all the other things, so she will look like an old-time Caddo woman. Has she moccasins?"

"Not yet," Mary answered. "I just got around to starting them."

"Let Alice make them," said the aunt. "I can show her how to cut and make the Caddo moccasins. Cheyenne moccasins wouldn't look right."

Jim traded work with a Delaware friend for a brown smoked deer hide, and for a few days the old aunt stayed with them, showing Alice, and Mary, too, how to make the soft-soled one-piece Caddo moccasins, with a checked pattern beaded on the toes and with beadwork bordering the dark blue velvet flaps.

The Fourth of July was there, all of a sudden, almost before they were ready for it. They drove out to the Agency in the buggy,

Josephine in her beautiful dress and jewelry, with the soft old paisley shawl folded over her arm. When they got there, Jim's aunt tied the hair ornament to the long braids hanging down Josephine's back, and the newspaper man came and took her picture. "I believe I'll have some postcards made up, too, if you don't mind," he told Mary. "It isn't every day you get to see a real Caddo costume like that."

Mary hesitated, but at last she gave him permission. Later, when she saw her girl's face smiling at her from the card rack in the drugstore, she was very proud. She bought a card and mailed it to Minnie, who had already bought one of her own, but was glad to have two anyway.

The three automobile dealers in Anadarko had each lent the Agency a brand-new shiny open car, with the top folded back, and the Cheyenne, Kiowa, and Comanche Princesses rode proudly, sitting on shawls spread on the canvas. Josephine rode with her school friend Augustine, the daughter of Mary's Kiowa friend, Maude Campbell, and they looked very lovely, sitting there in buckskin and satin. Augustine was older than Josephine, but that didn't make any difference. They were good friends, and their smiles and chatter brightened everything.

Alice and the old aunt rode in the buggy with Jim, in the part of the procession behind the Princesses, but Mary and Minnie took the old farm wagon and drove downtown. They found a good place to watch, on Broadway, in front of Jake's, and tied the horses to a hitching post. They sat there and watched the cars make the slow turn onto the Indian Main Street, and when Josephine and Augustine appeared they threw back their heads and shrilled the old victory cry, as if the girls had been young warriors returning from their first raid, and other women along the street took it up, so victory calls filled the ears of the whole town as one Princess or another passed her people.

Afterward, they went back to the Agency for a picnic, and the Agent made a speech about patriotism and loyalty and the flag, and they all tried to sing "The Star-Spangled Banner," but only Augustine, who was taking special singing lessons at school, could stay on the tune because everyone else sang Indian-style.

The next year other tribes wanted to take part in the celebration and to have Princesses. This time Josephine was elected Cheyenne

Princess, and wore her grandmother's old buckskin dress, with her hair falling loose, in the old way, over her shoulders and down her back. She wore the old German silver belt, with the great buttons set on rawhide—like a corset, it was so stiff. Jim gave her a pair of long silver earrings. Mary made her new moccasins, in the Sewing Women's striped design, with deer marching around the borders of the soles. She even beaded the soles, like those of a bride's moccasins. Minnie added a striped shawl for Josephine to fold over her arm. Until she was settled in the car, again with Augustine, Josephine wore her everyday shoes and carried the beaded moccasins in her hand. Then she changed, and handed the everyday shoes to her mother.

"Don't lose them," Josephine cautioned. "If I'm going to wear bride's moccasins, I will want to be carried like a bride, so they won't touch the ground."

Josephine was the child of Mary's joy. Not only had she wanted a girl from the first day she knew she was pregnant; she had dreamed of a girl like this one: sweet and beautiful and smiling. When Josephine graduated from high school the next year, and made what the principal called a valedictory speech, Mary was so proud she thought she would burst. It was all she could do to hold back the victory call when she saw her girl standing there in a white dress and heard her speaking so clearly in English.

Perhaps it was because of Augustine, who was attending the Eastman Institute of Music in Rochester, New York, that Josephine became more determined than ever to go to college that fall herself.

"Do you want to go with Augustine?" Mary asked her.

"No," Josephine replied, "I don't think I'd like it there. They all study music, and I'm not interested in that."

"What are you interested in?" Mary asked.

"I want to do something to help people," Josephine said seriously. "I want to be a teacher or a social worker, or something like that. I'd rather go to the Oklahoma College for Women in Chickasha."

"Then you'd better go there, if it isn't too expensive," Mary said.

"It won't cost very much," Josephine assured her.

Then Jim came up with an idea. "She can go to Haskell Indian school. It's in the same town as the University of Kansas, and she can get the first two years of college work at Haskell, with board and room free. Then she can go on living there and take her last two years at the University. I heard the Superintendent and the Educational Director talking about it the other day. It's a new plan the government has."

"I don't want her to go to Kansas!" Mary wailed. "It's too far away. At Chickasha she'd be near home. She could get back here once a week." She nodded her head, back and then forward, with determination. "I'll buy a car," she decided. "Then if I get too lonesome for her, I can go to see her."

"Buy a car!" Jim snorted, and Josephine supported him.

"Mother, you don't know how to drive," she protested.

"I'll learn," said Mary. "The Field Matron at the Agency will teach me. I'll take half the money I've been saving for your college, and work real hard to earn more money for your last two years."

Mrs. Peters, the Field Matron, agreed to the plan. "I was hired to make Indians progressive," was her decision, "and here's one who wants to be. Maybe she'll set an example for some others."

The lessons took place in an open field. Mrs. Peters had bought herself a farm west of town, because she was tired of living at the Agency and having other employees watching her. Every afternoon she drove the secondhand Ford Mary had chosen to the farm, where Mary and Josephine were waiting in the buggy, with the horse turned loose in a little pasture to graze.

When they were all three crowded into the front seat of the little car, Mrs. Peters explained the names of things, and what they were for. Then she slowly drove the car forward a few feet.

"Can you stop it?" Mary asked. Mrs. Peters demonstrated the brakes and how they worked. "And if you want to stop in a hurry, grab this handle and pull it back toward you," she instructed. "That's the emergency brake."

The next day Mrs. Peters said, "Now you try. I'll sit beside you, and if anything goes wrong I'll tell you what to do."

Gingerly, as if she were afraid the car would overturn, Mary crawled into the driver's seat.

"Josephine, you get down," she ordered. "I don't want anything should happen to you."

Josephine got out of the car, and stood where she could see her mother.

"Stand further off," Mary commanded. "I don't want to run you over."

"Now!" said Mrs. Peters, after Josephine had gone all the way to the pasture fence. "Try it, Mary. Turn the key and start the motor."

Mary obeyed. Under Mrs. Peters' directions, she put the car in gear, and they moved slowly forward, Josephine still watching them.

"Go faster," Mrs. Peters instructed. "Give it a little more gas."

Mary obeyed. The car surged forward. Josephine began to look apprehensive.

"Go on," said Mrs. Peters. It was the same exciting feeling as riding a good horse. Mary turned the car away from Josephine and out into the field. Then there was Josephine in vision again, still by the fence, but a little nearer this time. Mary turned the car away from her some more. The next circle brought Josephine still closer.

"Stop!" Mrs. Peters screamed. "Drive in a straight line. Stop!"

But Mary had forgotten how to stop. It was not until Mrs. Peters reached across and grabbed the emergency brake that the car came to a dead halt. Josephine had climbed the fence by this time, and was standing on its other side.

"You nearly did run me over, after all," she coolly observed.

"I guess I need some more lessons," Mary moaned.

"I guess you do," Mrs. Peters grimly remarked. "A lot of them."

So the lessons went on and on, until Mary had mastered the art of driving in a straight line, and the greater skills required to stay out of ditches and to rock a car back and forth to get it out of a mudhole when it was stuck. At last Mrs. Peters decided Mary was ready for the open road.

It was a dirt road, fortunately. There was no other traffic in sight, and Mary drove straight down the middle. By that time she had worn a driving track in the earth of the field, and the middle seemed the natural place to be.

And then another car came in sight, at a distance, and moving slowly.

"Pull over," Mrs. Peters snapped. *"Pull to the right!"*

Mary zigzagged across the road. She wondered why when you drove horses you always went to the left, but with cars it was just the opposite. Somehow, she got over to the right, and the two cars passed each other, going dead slow.

When it was over, Mary stopped and leaned her face against the wheel. "We made it," she said.

"We made it!" Josephine cried, and trilled the Cheyenne victory call.

"I never thought we would," Mrs. Peters said. They were all breathless with relief and excitement.

"I'll turn around and take you home," Mary offered, but Mrs. Peters shook her head.

"I'll walk," she announced. "It's only half a mile. You two go on home, now."

"I'll walk back with you and get the buggy," Josephine said, and the two left Mary alone, sitting in her car, wondering if she would ever be able to drive it again.

In the end, Josephine drove the car home. Mary, following in the buggy, wondered where the child had learned to drive. When the horse had been cared for and shut in the stable, with the car outside, Mary asked Josephine.

"Listening to you and Mrs. Peters, and watching you both," the girl answered matter-of-factly.

Jim just roared with laughter.

Josephine enrolled in the Oklahoma College for Women in the fall of 1935. The whole country seemed to be blowing away, and people talked of the "Dust Bowl" of western Oklahoma. But Mary had her money put away, and Josephine went to college as well dressed and well supplied as any other girl. Mary was proud of her.

One afternoon, when Mary visited Maude at the Agency, she found her friend laughing.

"Now we got another one," Maude giggled.

"Another what?" Mary demanded.

"Another anthropologist. This one's a girl, and she came here from Norman, from the University."

"How did you meet her?" Mary asked.

"They sent her over from the Agency," Maude replied. "She wants to study the Kiowas, she said. They told her I knew plenty of Kiowas, and could tell her the names of people who would work with her."

"Who did you think would be good?" Mary inquired. "Who did you send her to?"

"Oh, George and Lillian Hunt," Maude replied offhandedly. "George, he likes to talk. He knows a lot of the older people and can translate for her if she needs somebody. She's writing down the Kiowa history, she says."

"Seems to me everybody wants to write down Kiowa history," Mary said. "Mr. Mooney was out here doing that a long time ago, and then there was that Dr. Parsons, who hired Enoch Smokey's taxi because she couldn't drive, and Dr. Harrington, who wanted to write their language . . . been enough people studying the Kiowas. Why don't they study Cheyennes or Caddos for a change?"

"Well, I don't know," Maude answered. "I don't think this one will last long. She's as thin as a rail, and has the reddest hair you ever saw."

"How old is she?"

"About Augustine's age—a little older than your Josephine, I guess," Maude answered thoughtfully. "You never can tell with white people, you know. They all look alike—except for that red hair." She laughed again, thinking of the girl and her hair. "Maybe someday you'll meet her."

"Maybe," Mary said. What kind of family did that girl have, she wondered, to let her go off like that, away from home, with Indians? She shook her head. "I hope Josephine don't get any notions like that," she mused. "What good is an anthropologist, anyway?"

"I don't know," said Maude. "She says she's going to teach it in the University when she knows enough."

"How's she going to learn?"

"Listening to people. That's what she says."

Mary put down her coffee cup and rose. "I sure hope Josephine don't want to try it," she repeated.

But Josephine remained safely in Chickasha, studying home economics and how to teach it. Mary didn't have to worry about her Josephine! She heard about the anthropologist occasionally, through Maude. The young woman seemed harmless enough, and once Maude pointed her out on the Anadarko street. Mary again resolved to have nothing to do with her. Old times and history had come and gone, and she was living in today, going shopping at Levy's with Josephine and buying material for new school dresses.

All the same, Mary was curious about the girl. Perhaps it would be fun to sit down with someone like that and talk about old times. Nobody would want to hear the stories her mother had told her now but a girl who was interested in history. Maybe she would be interested, too, in the beadwork and moccasin making Mary herself had learned when she was young. Not even Josephine wanted the hard work of tanning, and when Mary got a cowskin for tanning nowadays, it was Jim who had to help her with the heavy work of stretching and pulling the hide.

13

❖❖

SONNY

Joe, Mary and Jim's second oldest son, had married a Caddo girl soon after he finished high school and moved to eastern Oklahoma, where he found a job as an automobile mechanic. In 1928 he returned with his wife and two sons—Clark, five, and Sonny, three—to live in a small house behind Mary and Jim's and work for a local garage.

Mary never told Jim but she had always worried about Joe, from the time he was born in the Fort Sill Indian Hospital. She had always known something bad would happen to him because he was born in a hospital. One spring morning about a year after they returned, she was surer than ever when Joe's wife came to Mary's kitchen door, tears running down her face.

"You pregnant again?" Mary asked.

"No," the Caddo woman choked out. "It's Joe. He's funny . . . again."

Mary was not surprised. People had already come to tell her of seeing Joe on the downtown streets, staggering drunk, or winding his way down back alleys from one blind tiger to another. Sometimes on payday he did not bring home enough money for groceries for his wife and two boys. Then Mary helped out.

The state was supposed to have had Prohibition since it came into the Union, but it was Prohibition in name only. It did not affect those well enough off to bring in liquor from out of state, nor those who were willing to buy from bootleggers. Joe had a good job as an auto mechanic; he worked well, and kept his mother's car running, when he was sober. But when he was drunk, which was more and more often, he was laid off, and threatened with losing his job for good. He was not destructive when he was drunk; he might be talkative, or he might just lie down anywhere and go to sleep. And nobody could be sure when this would happen.

Now his wife laid her head on the kitchen table and howled.

"You sound like a coyote," Mary observed impersonally.

The Caddo woman raised her head, tears still running down her cheeks. "I feel like a coyote—a mad one," she said. "I can't stand it anymore, Mother. I've got to leave him. He's over there now, sleeping, just sleeping. He doesn't know what I'm doing. He doesn't know what the children are doing. And he doesn't care. . . ." She drew a deep breath. "I can't stand it," she repeated. "I've got to leave. I'll move across town."

"What about the boys?"

"I can take the older one with me."

"And Sonny? What about him?"

"I give him to you."

So it happened that there was a child in the house again. Sonny was a sweet boy—gay and responsive and companionable to his grandparents. He was a blessing, Mary admitted.

When Sonny was six, his grandfather took him to school. He was enrolled in the first grade, for the town had no kindergarten. He was bright and made good grades, better than most Indian children, for he never heard anything but English spoken at home. Mary had great hopes for him.

Joe stayed on in the little house behind his parents'. He had managed somehow to buy it, and to pay the mortgage. Sometimes, when he had been working and was sober and had some money, he went to see his wife. Sometimes he lay soddenly on a dirty bed and snored. For one thing Mary was thankful: He never brought home any strange women. She did not have that shame to endure. Joe, himself, was enough.

Sometimes, when she was not busy, Mary took Sonny to see his mother. They would drive across town, Mary straight and apprehensive behind the wheel, and visit for an hour.

Sonny was all Mary's boy now. He and his school friends were young and alive and about the place, and Mary was thankful to have them. Like Josephine, too, Sonny was Cheyenne in appearance—tall for his age, with black, black hair. The only way you could have told he was not a full-blood Cheyenne was his eyes; like Mary's they were gray-blue. Otherwise, with his long bones and long face, he was all Cheyenne.

He surged through the kitchen door one summer day when he was ten, two of his friends behind him, and stopped facing his grandmother. "Cookies, please, Grandma?"

Mary reached for the package of vanilla wafers on the cupboard shelf and extended it. "Four apiece, now," she cautioned. "You could spoil your suppers."

The boys took the cookies, yelled "Thanks," and ran out again through the living room.

A moment later Mary heard a scream, a squeal of brakes, and a thud. Then silence. She ran through the living room and out into the street. Sonny lay against the curb, very still, with a car just backing away from him. The driver stopped, and Mary bent over Sonny.

A man she did not know came and stood beside her. "My God!" he said. "Oh, my God."

Mary clutched Sonny to her. "You've killed him," she gasped. "You've killed my boy."

"Let me take him to the hospital," the man offered. "I'll do anything. . . ."

Somehow Mary, tiny Mary, carried Sonny to the car and laid him across her lap on the back seat. The other boys stood watching, helplessly.

"Get word to the Agency, to his grandfather," Mary ordered them. "Tell him where we're going."

"Now," she said to the driver, and he started for the hospital.

Waiting was always the hardest part of anything bad. Mary had learned that long ago. Now she sat beside Jim, on the bench outside the operating room, while the two doctors and four nurses who staffed the city hospital were shut inside with Sonny.

At last one of the nurses came out.

Mary looked at her. "How is he?" she whispered.

"We think he'll live," the nurse answered carefully. "There is brain damage, though. His skull was broken."

Sonny lived. As soon as they were sure he would, Mary drove him to the Indian hospital at Lawton, with his mother sitting beside her, and Jim holding Sonny on the back seat. There they left him to rest and be watched.

Finally the word came. Sonny was well enough to come home now. So the three made the long trip again. It was only about thirty miles, but it seemed like three hundred. The trip back was even longer.

It was not Sonny they brought home with them. His neck was still in a metal brace, and the doctor told Mary it would have to remain so for several months, until his neck muscles strengthened again. The brace must have hurt Sonny, for he moaned and muttered and sometimes poked at it. He could not speak. Only Mary even pretended to understand him, and she was mistaken as often as not. Many times she gave him cookies when he wanted water, and the other way around.

Except for his neck muscles, Sonny was well enough physically. He ate and he grew, but there was no mind behind the blankly staring, light-colored eyes. And Sonny was very strong. One time he picked up a chair and broke it, a piece at a time, into kindling. The other children avoided him, but Sonny ran after them sometimes and once he caught one of the boys. There followed a bitter wrestling match that Mary only stopped with the garden hose.

Only Minnie and Robert came near them during that first terrible year. At its end, Mary took Sonny back to Lawton, and the doctors examined him again. They took the brace off his neck, and he could hold up his head now, very stiff, but straight.

"It's no use, Mrs. Inkanish," the chief doctor said, finally. "He'll never speak and he'll never be able to think clearly again."

"That's not true!" Mary cried. "He can dress himself and feed himself. . . ." She stopped, trying to think of any other accomplishments.

"Did you teach him?" the doctor asked.

"I did. All by myself. Like I would any baby."

"That's just it," the doctor said. "He can learn the things a baby learns, but nothing more. From now on, he'll be a walking vegetable. Is he strong?"

"Oh, very strong. He can outrun all the boys on the block. He even wrestles with them sometimes and I have to stop him. He drinks his milk, that's why he's strong."

"Does he mind you?"

"Yes. Nobody else, but he minds me."

"Be careful, then," the doctor warned. "If he gets too strong and doesn't mind you, we may have to send him away."

"Where to?"

"The state mental hospital. It's the only place where he can get the care he needs."

A day came when Sonny did not mind. He turned on Mary, yelled at her, and slapped her. Joe heard her scream and, cold sober for once, came running to the rescue. He struck Sonny a boxer's blow on the chin, and before his son opened his eyes again, Joe tied him hand and foot like a calf. Then they telephoned Lawton, and the hospital there made the arrangements at once.

"'He could kill you," Joe said, and Mary nodded.

All the same, she herself drove Sonny to the state hospital. He loved to drive with her, and was so good all the way that she wondered if this was not the wrong thing to do for him. Joe, on the back seat, must have read her mind, for he said at once, "It's all you can do, Mother."

And when Sonny saw the hospital and the white-uniformed attendants and began to scream and pound on the car windows, Mary knew that her son was right, and that there was only one thing to do.

Mary never drove a car again.

14

◇◆◇

THE WOMEN'S HEART CLUB

Mary and her sister-in-law, Alice Cussen, Laura Pedrick, and Dorothy Kawaykula, an Apache from out of town, sat on Maude Campbell's front porch at the Agency. Mary and Laura, who were always busy, sat at a table where their supplies could be laid out and made beadwork: Mary, a pair of moccasins, and Laura, a feathered fan. They sat in the easy silence of Indian women, broken by an occasional comment from one of them.

"There comes Martha Thomas," Mary said, pointing toward the Kiowa woman with her lips.

"I wondered when she'd show up," said Maude crisply.

"She might not get here," said Mary. "Walking, always walking. Like a white woman. You'd think we had no cars or horses."

Martha made her way across the oval of grass in front of the Agency and joined them, sitting on the porch steps.

"Sure hot," she informed the group.

Again they sat in easy, comfortable silence. Again Mary looked down the drive.

"My!" she said, "that Mrs. Peters sure got fine horses. A good wagon, too."

"Those ain't like the Gov'ment horses used to be," Dorothy pointed out.

"She buys her own," Maude added. "She's been buying them since her husband died, before she came here as Field Matron."

Mrs. Peters swung down from the wagon, tied the lines to the hitching rack, and entered the Agency building without looking to right or left. Her small, trim figure, even in her loose dress, might have been a girl's. Her wide-brimmed hat hid her features and the color of her hair, but she was unmistakably a white woman.

It was almost an hour before Mrs. Peters emerged from the Agency. Maude, as owner of the porch, stood up and called to her. "Come on over here, Mrs. Peters. We're making lemonade."

Mrs. Peters walked briskly toward them, and Laura and Maude went into the house.

It was not long before Maude reappeared with the lemonade and some store cookies. Mrs. Peters had settled herself at the table by Mary. Mary looked at her and a thought came to her mind. "I'd like to learn to knit," she said. "I could make a sweater for Jim. He fusses, fusses all the time. He says he is cold."

"You can learn," said Mrs. Peters. "Anyone who can make moccasins and beadwork can learn to knit."

"I wish I could sell more moccasins and beadwork," Mary answered. "I could help Josephine more."

Mrs. Peters looked surprised. "Do you mean you can't sell all that you can make at Mohonk Lodge?"

"That's right," Laura added. "We have to make them as they are ordered. If we use different designs the Lodge won't buy them. Then we have to sell them to Jake or give them away."

"He doesn't pay enough anyway," Mrs. Peters snapped. Between her and the pawnbroker there was perpetual war. "I tell you what," she went on, "I'll teach you to knit if you want to learn. We'll make a crafts society, and buy our materials together, so it won't cost anyone too much at one time. And then I'll write around, to people I know, and sell the things. We'll do our own selling instead of depending on Mohonk Lodge and Jake."

"A society?" Mary's eyes were bright. "Like in the old days. My people—Cheyennes—we had a special society for women who did fine beadwork. Only the ones that were good enough could join. They had to work hard, hard, to make things pretty."

"That's interesting," Mrs. Peters said.

"My mother belonged. It was a secret society. I never belonged, as most of the women had died when I was old enough. But my mother taught me about it and the designs. We can make a new beadworking society."

"What would we call it?" Alice asked.

"Oh, I don't know. Maude, what do you think?"

"Call it Women's Heart Club," Laura suggested. "That sounds pretty in Kiowa, *Mah-taym,* and a club is more modern than a society."

"We got three Kiowas and three other tribes," Martha put in. "That means the Kiowas can outvote the others, like they say."

"You get three Kiowas you got four different ways to do things." Dorothy chuckled. It was an old saying. They all knew it from childhood.

"Well, I'll vote with the others, then," Mrs. Peters remarked. "That way, maybe we can handle the Kiowas."

"You like that name?" Laura persisted. "Women's Heart?"

"I like it," Mrs. Peters agreed. She glanced around the porch. "How about the rest of you?"

One by one, in Indian fashion, they nodded agreement. Had there been any difference of opinion, another name would have had to be found. Consent had to be unanimous even though they voted—the majority never won.

"When will you start writing letters?" Mary asked.

"Tonight, when I get home. Oh, I think this will be a big thing! If people like the idea, we can take trips—go to Gallup for the Indian Ceremonial; maybe—maybe go east. Someday, maybe, it will be everywhere. But it started right here, with us women sitting on a porch drinking lemonade."

They had never seen Mrs. Peters so excited. Her usually sallow little face was flushed; she seemed to come alive, sitting there. "I haven't been so happy since my husband was taken," she said almost in a whisper. "We can get the young people interested in the old arts and crafts," she went on. "That would be a wonderful thing. They would be proud to be Indians."

"Why you say that?" Alice queried. "Everyone else say Indians different, got to be like white people to get ahead."

"To get ahead in the white man's way, maybe. But don't you see this is getting ahead in an Indian way? This is bringing back something good from the old times."

"Maybe," Alice said, hesitantly. "We try, anyway."

"Where we get beads?" said Laura, going straight to the heart of the matter.

"I'll order them from New York," Mrs. Peters said.

"Where will we get money?" Maude demanded. "We have to have money to put up when you order."

"I'll put up the money," Mrs. Peters said. The others were silenced. They all knew that, except for her horses and their care, Mrs. Peters lived as simply as any of them. It had never occurred to them that she might have money from anything but her Field Matron's salary, and they all knew that it was small. "I've got money in the bank back in Kentucky," she said now. "It was left to me. I'll draw some of it out to buy the beads."

It was a month until the beads finally arrived. Then the six women gathered in Alice's sitting room to open the package. Mrs. Peters had sent word to Dorothy, and she had come up from Apache to join the others for this great moment.

And great it was. The colors of the tiny Italian beads were true, the beads themselves evenly drilled and sorted. The women had never seen so many or such fine beads in one place before, not even at Mohonk Lodge.

The members of the Women's Heart Club worked hard. The work was slow with the tiny beads. It took Mary, who was a fast worker, at least a week to bead a pair of moccasins. They also made beaded bags and belts, which Mrs. Peters sold to people from Boston to San Francisco and in between. Even though their eyes grew tired the women were happy at their work. This was not like working for Mr. Kincaide; they could use their own designs, and did not have to choose from a pattern book. They had a great feeling of freedom in their work for the Women's Heart Club.

Besides, they were working for something they all wanted: a trip along dusty Route 66, westward to Gallup, New Mexico, where they could show their work along with that of other tribes; where they could dance and sing and feast in the Indian village the Chamber of Commerce of Gallup would provide for Indian exhibitors. They could make new friends.

The next great day came two years later, in 1936, when there was enough money in the treasury for the original members of the group, including Mrs. Peters—they would not have gone without her—to go to Gallup for the Intertribal Ceremonial. James Kawaykula, James Inkanish, and Robert Cussen went, too, and when they got to Gallup the men sang and drummed and the women danced. All the Navajos and Apaches and Pueblos and Hopis were surprised at the buckskin dresses and the fringes and the beadwork. They had never seen anything like it before. The people from Oklahoma had never seen anything like their costumes, either. Oh, it was fine!

Coming home, Mary broke a long silence to say to Mrs. Peters and the others who were riding in the car, "I guess it's pretty good, that Women's Heart Club. I guess people will remember us and talk about us for a long time to come. We're different tribes, but we are all Indians. I guess we make Mrs. Peters Cheyenne. Adopt her."

"No," said Maude. "You're one Cheyenne. We have lots of Kiowas. We make her Kiowa."

And so it was done.

15

THE INDIAN
ARTS AND CRAFTS BOARD

The Women's Heart Club hung together, even after Mrs. Peters retired from the Indian Service in 1937. Times were still hard; money was tight, they said, in the East. Not as much went into Washington in taxes, or came out in the form of education and health funds for the Indians. Drought still walked the Plains, and even those who were willing to farm could not do so. Dust from the once-plowed lands piled in dunes along roadsides and fence lines, and sometimes parents went hungry so they could feed their children.

Mary and Jim gave food to every child they could find who needed it, and Minnie and Robert did the same.

One night Minnie called on the telephone. "Mary," she shrieked, trying to make sure she was heard over the miles between Colony and Anadarko, "I want you and Jim to come up here Saturday. John Fletcher is putting up a big peyote meeting and a feast. I told him I'd help him out with the food if he'd pray for Sonny."

Pray for Sonny! As if any prayers could help him now! He was a good patient, the doctors said, quiet and obedient and sweet-tempered. He did not speak, but he could make gestures for what he wanted. He was beyond prayers, Mary thought. All the same she answered, "I'll come, Minnie. At least I can help you with the cooking."

"Thanks, Mary," Minnie shouted back, "I can use all the help I can get. And I want you to go into the meeting, too, even if it isn't your belief."

"What is?" Mary asked, and she repeated the question to herself, in one form or another, all week. Not the old Cheyenne religion, with its fasting and singing and dancing and medicine bundles, she was sure. Not the Sun Dance. She would never be able to forget that, or her mother's part in it, faraway as all that seemed now. As for the white man's religion, there were so many churches all arguing and quarreling among themselves. Perhaps peyote might be the answer for her, as it had been for Minnie. She would try.

So she asked Joe to drive them to Colony on Saturday morning and come back for them the next afternoon. She would pay for the gasoline, she told him.

"Okay," Joe agreed, and while he was getting the tank filled, Mary packed a basket with meat and bread and pink cakes she had gotten at the grocery the day before. When Joe came back, smelling only a little of cheap bootleg whiskey, she and Jim were ready to go.

Joe picked up the basket while Mary took the little tin suitcase that held her change of clothes.

"You must be fixing to feed the whole tribe," Joe said with a grin as he hefted the basket. "I thought Minnie and John Fletcher were putting up the meeting. That means they feed you, not the other way around."

"It isn't polite not to take a gift when you go visiting," Mary answered stiffly.

Minnie and Robert put up Minnie's tipi, in which the meeting would be held, northwest of their house where there was a slight rise.

It was a big meeting. Minnie's tipi was large, and as many as thirty people had already gathered when they entered. The priest was an old, old man, very bent and stooped and shrunken. He led the line of worshippers four times around the outside of the tipi, east to south to west to north, and back to the door, which faced east, before they went in. Then he seated himself on a bed of sage and quilts, like the one in the Sun Dance lodge, and the men and older women filed behind him and took their places on the north side.

The younger ones sat on the south side of the crescent-moon-shaped altar which enclosed a small fragrant cedar fire. People had come from many tribes. Mary, sitting with the older people on the north side of the door, looked across at George and Henry Tsoodle and George's wife, Margaret; they were all Kiowas she knew. Seated between George and Margaret there was a young white woman, a little older than Josephine. Her head was bent forward, like the other women's, but presently her shawl slipped back and her bright red hair picked up the light of the fire. Mary had seen red hair before, but never any as red as this.

"She looks like a hummingbird," she whispered to Minnie.

"That's what the Kiowas call her," Minnie whispered back. "The Hummingbird."

"What's she doing here?"

"She wants to learn Kiowa ways. George asked if they could bring her, and Robert said yes. That old man, he's putting up the meeting. He adopted her for his niece. He's Margaret's uncle. So he put up this meeting with John Fletcher and me, to show her to the people."

"You didn't tell me any of that before."

"I thought you wouldn't come if I did."

"What's her English name?"

"Alice."

"Ahneece." Mary had given up on *l* sounds long ago. "Ahneece. Like Jim's sister. What's her last name?"

"I don't remember the rest of it. It's a hard name, with *r*'s in it," said Minnie.

They sat through the night, to the singing and praying, the shaking of the rattle, and the soft tapping of the drum. All of them, including Alice, ate the required four peyote buttons. The white woman sat straight and still, not nodding or drowsy like some of the other young people. You had to respect her for it. If she wanted to learn Kiowa ways, she was willing to go through a lot to do it.

In the morning, when the water bucket was passed around, Alice drank from it like everyone else. She ate the ceremonial food—dried meat, corn, and fruit—from the common bowl with the common spoon. Mary, who had heard Mrs. Peters say for years that one of the worst dangers of peyote meetings was contagion from shared eating and drinking, was astonished. This woman didn't seem to be afraid of germs at all.

Alice worked with the other women to prepare the noon dinner, and ate with the younger women when the elders had finished. She had good manners. George and Margaret had taught her well. Why did she want to learn Kiowa ways? Mary wondered. Why not Cheyenne? They were just as good, maybe better, than the Kiowa ways of doing things.

After Mary got back to Anadarko, she forgot about the white woman. She was busy with her beadwork and housekeeping. The Principal at Riverside Indian School asked her if she would teach beadwork to some of the girls there, and Mary protested.

"All my life people been telling me the Indians should forget about beadwork. Only a few women left who do it well. Why do you want me to teach it, all of a sudden?"

"The Government has decided the Indians should learn all about their old ways," the Principal replied.

"First they take them away from us and now they ask us to teach the children," Mary remarked tartly. "What they want us to do next? Go back to wearing blankets and living in tipis? No buffalo left to make tipis now, anyhow."

The Principal laughed out loud.

"They're bringing back the buffalo, too, Mary," he said. "You know that wildlife refuge down near Lawton—west of Fort Sill. Well, they brought in about a dozen poor scraggly ones from a zoo in New York a few years ago, and now they've got so many they have to sell them off to other zoos and refuges."

"Well!" said Mary. She thought a moment, then asked, "Can they bring back deers, too, so we can make clothes?"

"They're already doing that in Arizona," said the Principal. "Things are getting more Indian every day. The Government has even set up an Arts and Crafts Board in Washington, to help the Indians all over the country sell the things they make."

Mary made her decision. "If they will help us sell things, that's good. I'll teach your students. Reese Kincaide, at Mohonk Lodge, he's getting pretty old to have to do it all." She thought a moment. "Where we get the beads for that beadwork I'm going to teach?" she demanded. "Who's going to pay for them?"

"I'll buy the first ones from Kincaide out of school funds, and you'll be paid for your time out of school funds, too," the Principal told her.

"I be paid?" Mary's chin went up. "That's good. In the old days, even when I was a girl, you had to pay the woman who taught you something." Another thought struck her. "Those girls at the school, they're mostly Kiowas. Only one or two Cheyennes. Maybe you better have a Kiowa teach them."

"Who?"

"Maude Campbell would be good. She's in our Women's Heart Club, but we are not doing much right now so she'll have time to teach."

"Tell you what," the Principal said. "You teach them Cheyenne beadwork and Maude can teach them Kiowa. We have enough money right now in the arts and crafts fund to pay you both."

All that fall and winter, two days a week, Maude picked up Mary at her house and they drove over the shaky wooden bridge across the Washita to Riverside School. There they worked, showing the girls how to split fine threads of sinew from the slab of backbone muscle of a cow that had been butchered at the slaughterhouse, and how to thrust their awls through the skin diagonally, so no stitches showed on the inside. They began with simple strips and patterns, and went on to make more complicated ones. When graduation time came in the spring, the girls had done enough good work to put on an exhibition.

Some of the older women came and looked, and admired.

One, boldly, asked Maude, "You teach me, too?"

"If you pay me," Maude answered.

But there was no money to pay to teach anybody, no money to get beads and sinew for them. The plan had to be dropped for the moment; even the children would not be taught the following year.

It was in the early spring of 1937 that Mary heard a knock at her front door. She saw a white woman with flaming red hair standing there. She opened the door and saw that the woman was a little older than Josephine, but she was taller and thinner.

"Mrs. Inkanish?" she asked.

"Yes. You that anthropologist I've been hearing about?"

"Yes, I'm Alice Marriott. May I come in?"

"Yes," Mary replied, and she held the door open wider.

They sat down in the neat living room. No one said a word for a while, until at last Mary asked, "Why are you here?"

"I've been appointed the Field Representative for the national Indian Arts and Crafts Board for the area of Oklahoma," Alice replied. "The Principal at Riverside School told me that you know a lot about Indian crafts. That you were willing to teach them at the school. Would you be willing to teach them at other schools?"

Mary thought a moment. "I don't know," she answered. "People I have taught have seen beadwork all their lives; perhaps these others would not know so much about it."

"Perhaps they would like to learn."

"Perhaps they would," Mary added. "I would be willing to try. Let us work together if we can. Is that what you mean?"

"That is what I mean," Alice said. "I've always wanted to work with Indians, all my life. I have begun with the Kiowas but that does not mean I must stay with them for always. The Arts and Crafts Board can pay you for your time."

"That is good. Then I'll have some money to help my daughter, Josephine. She goes to college. She goes to the Oklahoma College for Women over in Chickasha. She is in her third year. She wants to be a teacher.

"Come on." Mary got up and led the way back into the bedroom where her trunk was, and opened it. On the bed she laid fine tanned skin and sinew and beads.

"These things are what we use," Mary said. "Look at them. These are all of them that I have left, and I used to have a lot. The school ran out of money and can't buy any more or pay the teachers."

"Perhaps we can get you some. Perhaps we can organize an arts and crafts cooperative so we can buy these supplies for the people."

"Maybe we can," said Mary thoughtfully. "Do you think we can get deerskin and sinew again?"

"I think we can get deerskin from Arizona and the Dakotas. We will have to write letters and talk to people about these things. Beads, I'm sure, we can get in New York."

"Let's try, then," Mary urged. "If we work together we will do it well."

And so began the partnership that was to last the rest of Mary's life and to change the world for both of them. Together they visited the homes of Cheyenne women Mary knew and talked to them about the possibility of organizing a cooperative. Alice told them that if the women all pooled their money, what little they had, they could buy more beads as a group than they could as individuals. Mary knew that from the Women's Heart Club.

The Forest Service sent them dry deer hides, rolled—old some- times, but deer hides, and Mary began to teach the other women how to tan them. Sinew was harder to come by, but the butcher shop came to the rescue, and they managed to get enough cow sinew to stitch moccasins.

One day when they were together, Mary laid out a deer hide on the dining room table. "Do you know how to measure for moc- casins?" she asked Alice.

"Show me. Please."

"No," Mary told her. "You must learn to do for yourself. You must think how you would do it if you had no measure. No stick even to tell the size of the moccasins you were going to make. All you had was the pattern of the person's foot."

"I think I would do it this way," said Alice, and she laid her hands on the hide, one on either side of the back spine. "I would take from the tip of the middle finger to the bone of my wrist. I think it would be almost the length of my own foot." She slipped off her shoe and the idea worked. It was an accurate measure.

"How many pairs of moccasins can you get from a hide?" Mary asked.

Alice put her hands together and together and together four times, and she said, "I can get four pairs of women's moccasins from this hide but there will be some skin left over."

"What will you do with the rest?" asked Mary.

"I'll cut it up for baby moccasins," Alice replied. "But I will still have some left."

"With that what will you do?" Mary inquired.

"I think that I'd use it for string."

Mary threw back her head and laughed. "She is Cheyenne al- ready," she cried. "She knows what a Cheyenne does with buck- skin when she has it."

Then Mary showed Alice how to cut the string going from the

outside of the piece of hide to the inside with a pair of scissors, making it an even width all the way around. It was quicker than cutting with a knife, but Alice wanted to learn with a knife. They laid the hide out on the ground and cut strings against the earth. These would be ties for the moccasins.

"Now, what about the soles?" Alice asked.

"The soles are rawhide and you have the person's foot pattern," Mary answered. "The rawhide from a steer would be heavier and stronger than buckskin, so you would have to make it larger than the buckskin upper if you don't want the upper to pull loose from the sole and if you want the moccasin to fit right. You would cut around the outside of the pattern."

Again they spread a hide, this time a rawhide, on the ground, and this time they used a knife to cut around the outside of the pattern of Alice's foot.

"But where will there be a place for you to sew?" Mary asked. "What will you do about that? If you leave the sinew stitches raw they will rub your foot and hurt."

"Should I put the strip of buckskin string between the upper and the sole?"

"That's what the Cheyennes do," Mary replied.

She showed Alice how to put the strip of buckskin string between the upper and the sole, making a welt in the moccasin, and leaving two tabs at the back where the ends of the strings came together, where there would be just enough of the dangling buckskin string to wipe out the tracks of Alice's feet as she walked on the ground.

Teaching Alice to sew took a long time, but they did it. Mary made Alice rip out every wrong stitch as she made it. They went over and over that pair of moccasins until Alice said laughingly that there would be nothing left but a sieve and they would have to cut the moccasins down into children's moccasins.

"No," said Mary seriously. "You must not do that. Do not waste anything, you can wear them for everyday. We won't bead them, you know." And so it was done. Alice did wear the moccasins for a long, long time, until the soles wore out completely and the uppers split along the extra holes that she had made when she passed through the welt.

Bit by bit, one step at a time, she learned to tan. She learned to scrape rawhide. She learned all of the hard, heavy, dirty work the Cheyenne women had done in the old days. Mary watched with pride, which she did not show, and enjoyed the work and companionship. Other women came and took part in the work, and it was like the old-time days when women got together and helped each other with tanning and buckskin scraping for days at a time. In the evenings they did their beadwork.

16

TAHLEQUAH

About a month after that first visit, Alice said to Mary, "The Arts and Crafts Board is planning a summer school to teach crafts. Would you like to come and be one of the teachers?"

Mary hesitated. "Where would that school be?"

"In Tahlequah, at the Indian school there. Near Muskogee."

Again Mary pondered. "It's a long way off, isn't it?"

Jim had come into the room. He smiled his kind smile, at the two of them, so earnestly discussing the distance.

"You told me once, Cheyennes always travel, travel—Montana to Oklahoma and back again," said Jim. "Maybe to Colorado for tipi poles. You have old stories about the Mississippi River and the Glass Mountains. I've been hearing them since we were married. Now you wonder if you want to go two hundred miles. You'd still be in Oklahoma!"

Mary's chin came up, sharp and determined. "I'm not a Caddo," she said. "I don't have to stay in one place and farm. All right, Ahneece. We'll go."

"I'll stay here and take care of the garden," Jim said. "I don't mind. Josephine will be here to take care of me."

"Someday I'll take you both off somewhere and show you what it's like to travel," Mary retorted. "This time I'm going alone, with Ahneece."

"We'll need things to work with," Alice reflected. "We have sinew and beads. I'll have to try to get some hides."

"Get brains and liver, too," Mary reminded her. "Cheyennes say every hide has brains enough to tan itself."

"Can you be ready in a week?" Alice asked.

"Next Monday? Sure; I'll be ready."

So on Monday morning they started out, Mary with her little tin suitcase that always held her tools and materials for work, and a larger one for her few dresses.

After they had told everybody good-bye—Mary pressing her cheeks against Josephine's and Jim's in a special burst of emotion—and were in the car, headed east, Mary began to ask questions. It was unlike her; she usually waited to see what would happen, and then did what seemed best to her, but this was all so new that she was curious.

"What kind of Indians go to this school?" she inquired.

"Cherokees, mostly," Alice answered. "Some Creeks, Choctaws, Seminoles, but mostly Cherokees. The students are orphans, or they came from homes where they have only one parent. Each of the Five Civilized Tribes has its own school, but some from all of them go to this one. Except the Chickasaws. They have their own school at Ardmore, and they all go there."

Mary thought that over. "Why don't they get some of their own women to teach them tanning?" she demanded.

"They haven't done any tanning for a long time," Alice replied. "They've forgotten how to do it. That's why they need you."

Mary snorted. "They can't never tan like Cheyennes, even if they do try. I can show them and teach them, but they won't do it right after I leave.

"Did you get those hides?" she asked abruptly.

"It's the wrong season for buckskin," Alice reminded her. "They're sending some goatskins from the Navajo reservation, and I got some cowhides from the slaughterhouse in Oklahoma City."

"Don't smell them," Mary observed.

"They went up by truck Saturday," said Alice. "They're too big for the car, even if they didn't smell."

It was a long trip. They stopped for lunch in Okemah, and afterward walked down the street from the hotel to the post office, to see the big mural of the first Intertribal Council at Muskogee. Acee Blue Eagle had painted it. He was a friend of Josephine's.

"It's sure big," Mary remarked when she looked up at the wall, "but he's got the Cheyennes all wrong. Anybody would know he was Pawnee, the way he paints Cheyennes."

"Pawnee and Creek," Alice reminded her. "His father was a MacIntosh."

"Just as bad," Mary said, and stalked out of the post office.

Back in the car, she reverted to the subject of tanning. "If those people don't think enough of their tanning to keep it up, why do we have to teach them?" she inquired.

"We don't *have* to," said Alice, "but the General Manager of the Arts and Crafts Board thinks it's a good idea for all Indians to learn from each other."

"What do they make for themselves?"

"Pottery, and some basketry."

"Do I have to learn how to do those things? I saw a woman make pottery once. She came from New Mexico to the Anadarko Fair. I don't think I'd like to do that. She got mud all over her hands."

"No, all you have to do is teach tanning."

A sudden thought struck Mary. "If I teach, do I get paid, like the government teachers?"

"Oh, my goodness!" Alice exclaimed. "I forgot all about that. Of course you get paid. One dollar and fifty cents a day, and your board and room."

It was late when they got to the school—after seven. Supper was long over. Alice went to the Principal's house to ask about their rooms.

"You'll be in one building, and I'll be in another," she informed Mary. "I think even before we unload we'd better drive into town and get some supper."

"That's good," Mary said. "Lunch was so long ago my stomach forgot it had one."

They found a little restaurant on the main street of the town, and there they consumed chicken-fried steak, milk gravy, mashed potatoes, and canned green beans. They had a choice of coffee or iced tea, and both chose the latter.

"Just like Anadarko," Mary remarked when she finished. "Only place you can get food that tastes like anything is at home."

Alice sighed, thinking how many such meals she had already eaten, and how many probably lay ahead of an Arts and Crafts Board Field Representative. "Let's go back," she urged. "We ought to get settled for the night."

They drove back in silence, and stopped first at the Employees' Club so Alice could check her room assignment. A man and a woman sat in rocking chairs on the front porch. The man stood up when the car stopped. He was the tallest man Mary had ever seen— taller than a Northern Cheyenne, taller than a Crow wearing a headdress.

"Mrs. Inkanish, this is Mr. d'Harnoncourt, General Manager of the Arts and Crafts Board," said Alice.

"And this is Miss Morrow," he said. "Mrs. Inkanish, Miss Marriott—Miss Morrow." His English was funny, more broken than Mary's own, but in a different way. Afterward she learned that he came from a country overseas—Austria.

"You're going to room with me," Miss Morrow told Alice. "That's why we were waiting for you. We began to get worried."

"We went into town to get supper," Mary remarked. "Now you take me to my room, Ahneece. We all get a little rest. Morning comes too soon."

In the morning, for Mary, it was like being back at school herself. The rising bell rang at six and the breakfast bell at seven. By that time Mary had made her bed, washed and brushed her hair, and put on a clean dress. She went down the stairs of the girls' dormitory, where she had a room intended for ten all to herself. Alice met her in front of the building.

"You better move over here with me," Mary greeted her. "I got more room than you have, I bet."

"I'm all right," Alice remarked as they fell into step, side by side. "Miss Morrow's a good roommate. She's quiet and neat. Neater than I am," she laughed.

It was still school in the dining room. They all stood behind their chairs while the Principal said Grace, then sat down. There was a glass of orange juice and one of milk at each place, and a coffee cup mouth-down in its saucer beside them. Mary looked around, and her eyes settled on the Principal again.

"He looks like an Indian," she observed.

"His mother was Cherokee," Alice informed her. "He's a very nice man."

They passed scrambled eggs, bacon, and margarine around the table. There was a bowl of oatmeal, too, but that went back to the kitchen untouched at the end of the meal.

As they rose from the table, Miss Morrow came across to them. "You come with me, Mrs. Inkanish," she said in a voice so small it was almost a whisper. "I'll show you the work and supply rooms."

"Can Ahneece come, too?" Mary queried. She felt a little frightened, for the first time. Alice was her link with home, almost like a daughter.

"Mr. d'Harnoncourt wants her for some other work," Miss Morrow replied. "Come on with me; I'll take care of you."

"All right," Mary agreed, and they went away across the campus while Alice and Mr. d'Harnoncourt stood and watched them go and waved. Mary waved back. The waving made her feel more cheerful, somehow.

There were hides and beads in the storeroom. The cowskins were rolled up and dried out, as were the goatskins.

"Where do you want to work?" Miss Morrow asked.

"Got to work outdoors," Mary answered. "Can't work on hides in here. You got a creek around?"

The other teachers and some of the older students had gathered by this time.

"There's a creek right behind the girls' building," one student volunteered.

"We go there," Mary decided. "Everybody who wants to tan a hide, pick one out."

Most people chose goatskins, because they were smaller, but Mary noticed that Miss Morrow, like herself, took a cowskin. The class filed down to the creek.

"Now we find stones," Mary instructed them. "Good big heavy stones, four apiece."

The women scattered out, hunting up and down the creek banks. Some of the students followed the examples of Mary and Miss Morrow, who took off their shoes and stockings and waded into the deeper water, but most of the teachers stayed on the banks.

They were less successful than the waders in finding stones hard and heavy enough to weight down the skins.

"City folks," Mary snorted under her breath, and Miss Morrow shot her a smile.

When all the available heavy stones had been collected, they heard the lunch bell.

"We'll leave them here while we eat," Mary announced. If she was to be the teacher, she would have to tell them what to do.

It was a light lunch and they ate it quickly, before returning to the creek bank.

"Now we have to unroll the hides," Mary announced.

That proved to be easier to say than to do. The hides had been rolled so long, and were so dry and so stiff, that they could not get them unrolled.

"If we had some rope," Mary remarked thoughtfully, "we could tie them all together and put them in the creek and fasten the rope to a tree so they will not float away. If they soak overnight in the creek, they'll be easier to unroll."

"I'll see if I can find some," said Miss Morrow. "You come with me, Miss Roper," she added to one of the teachers.

"Get a butcher knife, too," Mary called after them.

After what seemed like a long time, but probably wasn't, the two women returned, carrying a coil of heavy rope between them. Miss Morrow held a butcher knife in her other hand.

"Where did you get them?" one of the students asked.

"We got the rope from the car repair shop, and Miss Marriott talked the cook out of the knife, but it's just a loan," Miss Morrow replied. "And Miss Marriott says, Mrs. Inkanish, that if you'll make a list of things ahead of time, it will be easier for her to steal them when she has to. Mr. d'Harnoncourt said so, too. He got the rope for us himself."

"I hope Mr. d'Ancou does not think she was joking," Mary retorted. "Ahneece, she'd say anything, but she'd do it, too."

It was late afternoon, and the shadows were stretching themselves along the creek banks, when they had finished making a hole in each hide, stringing them all together, knotted in place, and securing them to a tree. The knife was considerably dulled by then, but Mary sharpened it on a stone until you could hardly tell that it had had such hard use. They left the hides to soak overnight.

Mary took off the dress that had been so clean and fresh that morning, and that now showed how hard she had worked all day. She hung it on the back of a chair to dry, for it was soaked with creek water and perspiration, and put on a fresh dress. No use having more than one work dress. She'd have to find the school laundry, as it was.

"Everybody got to have a butcher knife," she told Alice. "Me and Miss Morow are the only ones that brought good knives. How they going to tan hides without knives?"

"I don't know," Alice replied. She looked at Mr. d'Harnoncourt, hesitating. "I can go into town and pick them out tomorrow morning," she went on. "Can the Board pay for them? I certainly don't want to face that cook again! You'd think her old knife was ruined!"

"I guess the Board can pay for the equipment for this project," he reassured her. "I'll go with you. I haven't seen this town yet, anyway.

"How many will you need?" he asked Mary.

"We got twelve women in the class," she answered. "Maybe you better get eleven straight knives, in case one breaks. Get a hoof knife at the saddle store, too. We can scrape the legs with that."

"A hoof knife?" Mr. d'Harnoncourt asked.

"A crescent-curved blade," Alice said. "Out-curved. It will go places a straight blade won't. You can use them for a lot of things: carving out spoons and bowls, and things like that, besides tanning."

They left for town right after breakfast, and when they came back, with eleven straight knives and an in-curved hoof blade as well as the out-curved one Mary had requested, they found that the two cowskins had been unrolled and were ready to stake out, but the women with the goatskins were still struggling with them.

"Goatskins sure are mean," Mary observed. "I guess those women thought they'd be easy because they're little, but I don't know. I bet we have a fight with them every foot of the way."

She and Miss Morrow smugly took their knives and began making holes around the edges for the stakes that would stretch their hides. The lunch bell rang.

"Seems like every time we get started we have to stop," Mary scolded. "You better string your hides together again and put them back in the creek while we eat."

"Oh, that reminds me. . . ." Mr. d'Harnoncourt started off across the grass ahead of the women.

"He got a new rope for the repair shop," Alice explained. "He said if he'd known what we needed, he'd have got it before. So he's going to replace this old one."

"You better tell him what we need next will be brains and liver and a pound of lard from the butcher shop," Mary remarked. "I know you can't steal them from the cook. Maybe she can let us put them in the refrigerator, though."

"I'll ask her about that," Miss Morrow offered. She really was the senior of the party, and the arts and crafts teacher at Haskell Institute, in Lawrence, Kansas.

The women who had been fighting with the goatskins looked tired, but Mary and Miss Morrow were as fresh as if they had just gotten up. After lunch, they went back to the creek. Alice came with them.

"When will you need the brains and liver?" she asked.

"Not for a while," Mary said thoughtfully. "We got to get these hides all stretched and scraped clean before we're ready for them."

It was a long, slow, hard week. Mary had tanned cowskins before, and she and Miss Morrow, who had once lived and worked in the Sioux country, knew what to do with them, but the goatskins were another matter. When the flesh that remained on the inside had been scraped away, and the hides turned over so the hair could be removed, they found that between the hair and the inner skin they wanted to tan there was a thin, transparent layer of another skin, so the goatskins had to be scraped three times.

"Like a wrapper on a cereal package," Mary remarked despairingly to Miss Morrow.

Some of the women gave up and said they would go to the pottery-making classes instead—tanning was too hard. Mary let them go. She was about ready to give up on the goatskins herself. But by Friday evening the last one had been scraped clean, and was ready to have the paste of brains, liver, and fat rubbed into it.

The stores in town were open that evening, and Mary and Alice made the rounds of all of them, collecting liver and brains at each and a pound of lard at the last one.

"Do you think we have enough?" Alice asked finally.

"I don't know," Mary said. "I don't know how them old goat-skins will act now. I hope I never see a goat again."

"Do you want to go into Muskogee with me tomorrow?" Alice inquired. "I have friends there, and they've asked me to spend the night. I know they'd be glad to have you, too, and we could go to some more butcher stores."

Mary pondered. "You go," she directed at last. "Get all you can. Miss Morow showed me where the laundry is, and they said I could use it tomorrow. I better, too. My work dress smells of goat."

"All right," Alice agreed. "I'll come back about four o'clock and we'll go into town to eat. They won't have anything here but cold bologna sandwiches."

"Just like all Government schools," Mary snorted. An idea struck her. "Maybe Miss Morow come too?"

"I'll ask her," Alice promised.

It was a woebegone Mary who met her on her return on Sunday. Tears were not falling now, but it was clear that tears had been shed.

"What's the matter?" Alice exclaimed, as she jumped from the car.

"Ahneece, Ahneece! I'm so glad you're back! That old cook! Miss Morow try to stop her, but no good. Ahneece, she say my brains are all spoil, and Ahneece, she throw my brains out! They got to spoil a little, or they don't work good."

"It's all right," Alice comforted her. "I have ten pounds each of liver and brains in the car, and we'll put them in the repair shop overnight, so they'll be just right. Did she throw out the lard, too?"

"No." Mary was openly weeping now. "She use it all up in her old tough piecrust."

"We'll get some more, then," Alice determined. "Come on. Wipe your eyes and put on a pretty, clean dress. Then we'll get Miss Morrow and go into town for supper."

"All right," Mary said, and went up to her ten-bed dormitory, a little comforted.

Mary never gave up, but in spite of her best efforts, the people of the Five Civilized Tribes never really learned to tan. Miss Morrow knew how already, and Alice learned easily enough, but the others only thought of it as hard, dirty work.

Mary was glad when the month was over and she could return home again, back to Anadarko, where people knew what tanning was all about.

17

◇⬦◇

CALIFORNIA, HERE I COME!

On the way back to Anadarko, Alice began to talk to Mary about next year's plans. She herself would be away most of the summer, but would come back to Anadarko as often as she could.

But the following year . . . ! The following year, 1939, Mr. d'Harnoncourt had told her, would be very exciting. There was to be a great Exposition in San Francisco, and the Indian Arts and Crafts Board had been asked to prepare an Indian display and a salesroom. The building that housed it would cover four acres. That Mary did not believe, even from Alice, but she kept her thoughts to herself.

"Would you like to go there as a demonstrator?" Alice asked.

"Not without Jim," Mary said firmly.

"What crafts work can he do?"

"He can make bows and arrows. Little ones for play toys; big ones for real shooting. He can make drums—makes best drums you ever heard."

"Hmmm!" said Alice. "I'll ask Mr. d'Harnoncourt. He might want someone to make those things."

"I don't go without Jim," Mary reiterated. "Been away from him too long this summer already."

During the fall, whenever Alice could get to Anadarko, they talked about it. Mr. d'Harnoncourt had agreed it would be a good idea to have someone to make bows and arrows and drums, so that was all right.

Letters went back and forth, all plans and plans and plans. The Navy had given them a barracks building on an island adjoining the one that was being specially dredged out of the shore of San Francisco Bay for the construction of the Exposition Building.

"What's an island?" Mary demanded when she heard that.

"A body of land entirely surrounded by water," Alice quoted from her sixth-grade geography book.

"I think I don't like that—all that water," Mary said thoughtfully, and Jim added, "Where they going to get it, anyway?"

"The water is *there*," Alice informed them. "San Francisco Bay is part of the Pacific Ocean, you see."

"What is it, that San Francisco?" Mary inquired. "Is it all water?" She was having second thoughts about making the trip.

"San Francisco is the name of the Bay, and it's the name of a city beside the Bay." Alice smiled. "You'll see. It's one of the most beautiful cities in the world."

"You been there?"

"Just once, coming back from my first field trip. I went to Oregon, and came home by way of San Francisco."

"Trees there?" Jim asked. "Flowers? Or just all that water?"

"Great big trees, and lovely gardens. Geraniums grow up to the second-floor windows of some houses. And there are beautiful stores, and good restaurants, and cable cars going up and down the hills, and Chinatown. . . ."

"Is everybody there Chinese?" Jim asked.

"Just in one part of the city. We'll go there, and you can see for yourself."

"Some people say Indians were Chinese once," Mary remarked. "Maybe we can find someone speaks our language. Who else be there? Just us?"

"Lots of people. Indians from all over the United States—Alaska, even. And Mr. d'Harnoncourt will be there, and Miss Morrow. . . ."

"That's good; I like them. Who else?"

"Well, Mr. Disher, he's Mr. d'Harnoncourt's assistant, will be there part of the time. And Mr. Douglas from the Denver Art Museum—you'll like him—and a whole lot of other people. And you'll be too busy to get lonesome, anyway."

It was Josephine who finally settled the matter. "What about you? Will you be there?" she asked Alice.

"Oh, yes. I'll drive them out and be with them every day till we're ready to come back."

"All right, they can go," Josephine agreed. "They have to have somebody they know real well, and I can't. Now I'm finishing college, and by next summer I'll be job hunting."

"They going to pay us?" was Jim's next question.

"You'll have your room and board in the Navy barracks," Alice said. "And they'll pay you each two dollars a day, and the profit from whatever you make and sell."

"Sounds pretty good," Jim decided.

"When do we start?" asked Mary, the practical Cheyenne traveler.

"The plan is for us to go out in late September, when the worst heat is over, and come home by Thanksgiving."

"Then we better start getting ready," Mary observed. "Here it is October this year already, and we got a lot to do."

From then on, they were absorbed in preparations. Mary tanned eight calfskins she got from the slaughterhouse, and made sure she had the right ingredients to make them soft and white. Jim helped her with the heaviest parts of the work, but he was busy too. He made several trips to Colony during the winter, and he and Robert Cross went through the grove looking for straight branches of dogwood and bois d'arc for arrows and bows. The drum frames they made out of cheese boxes Mary begged from the grocery, and she made up two rawhides for drum covers.

The pile grew and grew. Alice was in Michigan that winter, with Miss Morrow, working with the Chippewas and Winnebagos, and when she got back Mary showed her all they had accumulated.

Alice looked out at her little car and shook her head. "Where are we all going to *sit?*" she wailed. "The car just holds three people, and even if none of us is big we'll never get all that in, and ourselves, too."

"We find a place," Mary consoled her.

"I suppose I can have my big suitcase shipped out and just take the overnight bag," Alice said.

"Where are we going to stay?" Mary asked, practical as always. "Indian Schools?"

"No, motels. The Board's paying all travel expenses, you know."

"I never was in one of those places," Jim observed. "Any of them nice? This old one here's pretty bad, I hear."

"There are lots of nice ones on the highway, with their own restaurants," Alice informed him. "We can park the car right outside the door of my room, so I can hear if anyone tries to bother it in the night." She knew Mary worried because Jim's hearing was growing less and less keen.

"That's good," Jim agreed. "That's what we'll do."

The next morning Alice took her big suitcase to the railroad station, and with hope and fear, started it on its way. Then they began packing. Jim's wood took up the bottom of the trunk space, because Mary refused to let her hides and sinew go anywhere else but on the top of the load. Nothing was going to crush them.

Clark, Joe's older son, ran in and out and supervised everything as only a boy can. At last Josephine, who had returned home from Poteau, a good day's drive southeast of Anadarko, where she was teaching, made him sit beside her.

Finally it was all done. Every piece of working material, every tool, every box and bundle of clothing—even the overnight case— was wedged in somehow.

At the last moment Josephine came out with two large paper bags. "There's your lunch for the road," she said, handing one to her father, "and this is the buckskin dress for you to wear at the Exposition."

"I was saving Grandma's dress for you to be married in!" Mary cried.

"You wear it first. It's so pretty, people ought to see how good Cheyenne beadwork is. I wouldn't get married until you got back, anyway. I put in everything: moccasins, leggings, the belt— everything but a shawl. You packed that last night."

So they were on their way. From Anadarko to Gallup, New Mexico, the road was familiar to all of them.

"What state next?" Jim asked over breakfast the third day.

"Arizona," Alice replied, "and then California. We have two days' drive in that state before San Francisco. No, wait a moment," she corrected herself. "We will also take a side trip into Nevada to see Boulder Dam."

"I always did want to see that place," Jim remarked.

Mary was more interested in the turning gold of the mountain aspens. She struggled with the pronunciation of their name for a while, and then gave up. Forevermore, as far as Mary was concerned, they were "aspirin trees," and the state where she first saw them was "Ailizola."

Jim made fun of her pronunciation, and the trip turned into an exercise in linguistics: how Caddos said some things and how Cheyennes had different names for them. Then Alice contributed a scrap of her sparse Kiowa, and so they passed the time while the country around them flattened and grew bare and dry, with the friendly mountains and their lovely trees becoming a blue shadow on the horizon behind them.

They stopped for an evening meal, and went on into the gathering dusk. It was dark when they reached the first crossing of the California line. A state trooper stopped them, holding up his hand. Alice pulled into the roadside parking space he indicated. A line of other cars stood there already.

"Got any fresh fruit or vegetables?" the trooper asked.

"No," said Jim, taking the initiative, "we ate them."

"Any tree shoots, or plants of any kind?"

"Just my dogwood and bois d'arc sticks for making bows and arrows," Jim assured him.

"You'll have to get rid of them. Can't let you bring any plant material into California. We don't want to get borer beetles in the orange groves," ordered the trooper.

"But the perfectly dry wood can't start a borer infection," Alice objected. "These were cut last winter and they've been drying ever since."

"Have to inspect them," the guard reiterated. "Orders from the Department of Agriculture."

"We'll have to unload everything in the car!" Alice exclaimed. "Isn't there anyone to help us?"

In the beam of the headlights they could see that the people in the car ahead of them were eating oranges as fast as they could. The fresh smell drifted back to them, and Mary realized how tired and thirsty she was. "I'm going to get one," she announced.

They all got out of the car, and while Jim and Alice began to unload, Mary walked over to the other vehicle. She had never asked anyone for food before in her life, let alone strangers, but these people seemed to have lots of oranges and to be eager to get rid of them.

She leaned on the car door. "Sure smell good," she commented.

"I don't think they'll ever smell good to me again," said the driver. "Do you want some?" He held out a large paper bag, and Mary daintily selected three oranges.

"Oh, for pity's sake," said the woman on the other side of the front seat, "give her the whole bag, Tom. If any of us eat any more of them, we'll be sick. I *told* you not to take so many."

"Penny apiece in the groves near Tucson, if you pick them yourself," said the man. "All right, lady. You can have them. My wife's right. We will be sick if we eat any more."

"I pay you for them," Mary offered.

"I don't want to have to count them," the wife said. "I don't ever want to see an orange again. Take them. You're welcome to them."

"Thank you," Mary replied, and went back to the car. She peeled some for Jim and Alice, and the three of them grabbed bites in the intervals of piling their goods at the roadside. The car ahead of them got a quarantine-free sticker on its windshield and drove away. Mary waved, but her wave was not returned. By the time she finished her third orange, she understood why. Her stomach began to hurt.

Eventually, every stick of wood had been inspected, the oranges disposed of in a waste container, and a quarantine-free sticker attached to their windshield. The light of a town came in view ahead, and Alice announced, "I don't care where we are, we're stopping here."

The next morning they took the road north, and at noon they came to the little town near Boulder Dam. This was the big treat Jim had been looking forward to for two days. The land around them was bare of anything but sagebrush and creosote bush, and the temperature was as hot as an Oklahoma summer, but the sheer mass of concrete before them, with water coursing down its face into the basin below, held them all spellbound.

They walked across the top of the dam to the engineers' office. There a tour guide led them, with a group of other people, down a stairway and into a tunnel inside the dam. Mary thought she recognized the people who had given them the oranges the night before, but she could not be sure.

From station to station their guide led them. All the men asked endless questions about the workings of the dam, and all the women looked as if their feet hurt. Mary knew hers did. All that walking on pavement had tired them out. She longed for grass to walk on. This was harder than walking from Darlington to Colony, when she was a girl.

At the end of the tour they reached another stairway, and climbed up into daylight again. Back in the car, Jim shook his head and said, "That was sure wonderful. Thank you for it."

"You're welcome," said Alice. As for Mary, she could not, in good conscience, thank anybody for feet as sore as hers were at the moment.

The rest of that day they were still in desert country, but toward evening they came back to the California line again, and saw blue mountains and green trees, and felt refreshed. Their quarantine sticker let them through the highway inspection post without question or delay, and they went on to the next town.

Mary could never remember the names of the towns where they stopped for food or gasoline or to spend the night. One looked like the other to her. And then there was a big town ahead of them, and beyond it water, taking on sunset shades. A great bridge arched across the Bay.

"San Francisco?" Mary asked.

"Oakland," Alice said. "We drive across the bridge to the islands, and if we kept on it, we would be in San Francisco."

They drove through the outskirts of Oakland and out onto the great bridge. In the middle, there was a fork. Alice turned off to the left; ahead of them were the stark gray Navy barracks. An appetizing food smell greeted them when they stopped.

Miss Morrow was there waiting for them, and they all shook hands as if they were strangers, and then hugged each other like friends.

"I'll take you in and introduce you to the Matron," offered Miss Morrow, "and she'll show you where you will stay, and where the dining room is."

They were taken to pleasant sleeping quarters that overlooked the Bay. Green ferny trees with a wonderful pungent smell grew outside.

"What are those?" Mary asked.

"Eucalyptus trees."

"But eucalyptus is cold medicine."

"It comes from the oil from the seeds of those trees," said Miss Morrow. "I thought I'd drive back with you," she said, turning to Alice. "You wrote that your brother is in Berkeley, so I got rooms for us near the campus."

"Thank you; that will be nice."

"You don't stay here with us?" Mary wailed.

"We're not allowed to. Only Indians can stay here. You take tomorrow off and get rested from the trip, and I'll be over in the morning to see if you're all right," Alice reassured her. She turned to Miss Morrow. "Have you the hotel's name and telephone number?" she asked. "Then, if Mrs. Inkanish needs anything, she can call us."

Miss Morrow produced a slip of paper from her handbag. "I thought that would be the first thing you'd ask for," she smiled. "Here it is. I wrote it down this morning." She gave Mary the penciled slip, and shook hands again. "Good night. Get your dinner, and we'll see you in the morning," she instructed them, and led Alice away to the car.

18

THE CITY AT THE OTHER END
OF THE BRIDGE

There was lots of fun and excitement at Treasure Island—the new man-made island where the Exhibition was to be held. There were old friends, like María Martinez and her husband, Julian, who came to the Anadarko section of the Exposition to see Alice. There were new friends, like Sophie and Luke Big Turnip, from the Sioux country, to become acquainted with. Mary never felt very close to the Navajo family, the Lees, but that might have been because they kept pretty much to themselves. They had a little girl with them, about four, a pretty little thing, but she had had polio, and one leg was shortened and twisted.

There was Mr. d'Harnoncourt, of course, and sometimes his beautiful wife would come with him to spend a day at the Exposition. Alice was always there when Mary and Jim were, within call if they needed her. The demonstrators worked in one end of the salesroom, and Alice was behind the counter that ran along one side of it, so Mary had only to lift a hand to catch her attention.

In the evenings there was an almost endless stream of visitors coming and going at the barracks: people who knew Indians well and some who had never seen them before. A few Mary had heard of from Mrs. Peters because they were collectors of Indian art: Judge and Mrs. William Denman; Mrs. Margaretta Dietrich and her sister, Dorothy Stuart; and the trader from Gallup, New Mexico, M. L. Woodard. These were all new people she liked, and she was happy to meet them.

The first morning, Alice was waiting for them when the bus stopped in the courtyard of the building bringing the demonstrators from the barracks to the work area. Beside her stood a man almost as tall as Mr. d'Harnoncourt, whom she introduced as Mr. Douglas.

He shook hands matter-of-factly and said, "I hope we can all be friends."

Mary looked at him and answered, "I guess we will."

"Mr. Douglas takes people through the displays and explains things to them," Alice said. "We thought it would be a good idea if you spent the first morning going around with him in one tour group."

Mary had walked from Darlington to Colony when she was a girl, and that was a lot longer than walking around four acres, but she was tired and aching when the tour ended. She had seen and heard so much, she didn't believe she would understand it. There was the art of all the Indians in the United States at this show— tribes she had heard of and tribes she never knew existed.

They looked at the ivory-trimmed fur coats of the Eskimos, and they looked at the great feather-covered baskets of the Pomos, and then at feathered baskets so tiny they had to be shown under a microscope. There were coiled storage baskets from the Papagos almost large enough to hold a grown man. And there was one whole wall for the Plains tribes, with painted figures on horseback as a backdrop. Only, these figures wore real war bonnets, set so that a stream of air from a hidden fan blew their feathers into constant motion. Mary thought for a moment that she was back at home in the short-grass country, watching the real riders her mother had told her about.

"It's wonderful, just wonderful," Jim said, and she nodded in agreement.

Then they had lunch out of paper bags they had brought on the bus with them, sitting in the pale, thin sunlight of the courtyard. Alice and Miss Morrow joined them.

"How do you like it?" Miss Morrow asked.

"It's too big," Mary replied. "We'll have to see it some more, to understand all those things that Mr. Dougnas talked about."

"As often as you like," Alice assured them.

Lying on her narrow bed in the spotlessly clean barracks, Mary wondered about a lot of things. Would people really believe there were so many different kinds of Indians? Would they understand all the different crafts? Or would they think that some of them, like the Seneca and Cherokee masks, were ugly? She turned to speak to Jim, but he was already snoring.

That was one of the few evenings they had spent alone. As they became better acquainted with the other workers, they visited back and forth, from room to room. Sometimes, when they had special guests, they gave a dance to celebrate.

They danced for a man Mr. d'Harnoncourt said was the French Ambassador. He joined in the dance with them, but he danced all wrong, coming down hard when his feet should have been going up. A lot of white people did that. It made Mary giggle to watch them; they danced backward, like the backward-talking clowns of the Cheyennes.

Then there was a day when the whole exhibition hall was closed off, and the public could only come into the salesroom.

"Why they do that?" Mary asked.

"Mrs. Denman and some of the other ladies are going to take little Dolly Lee to the hospital, for an operation to straighten and strengthen her leg, but her old grandfather is a medicine man, and he wants to try the Navajo way first. They're making a sand painting now, to cure her."

"They make sand paintings every day," Mary reminded Alice. "People look at them all the time."

"They make mistakes on purpose in those sand paintings," Alice remarked. "But this is a real one, a sacred one, for curing, and no one can go in till it is finished."

"Not even the other Indians?" Jim demanded.

"Not even them," Alice reiterated. "Wait till sundown. Then we can go in when they tear it up and rub it on the little girl to make her well."

"Seems like a lot of work, just to tear it up," Jim observed, "but I guess they got their own ways."

Just before sundown, the bus drove into the courtyard, and the old medicine man came out of the hall. "You wait here," he ordered the driver. "All the Indians can come in now."

"I don't go without Ahneece," Mary declared. "I don't feel right without her."

So a few of the white people were allowed to go in: Mr. d'Harnoncourt, Mr. Douglas, Miss Morrow, and Alice. They stood quietly with the Indians. The sand painting of the Wind Singer's Chant was very beautiful, with the four wind goddesses framing it. Little Dolly and her mother sat in the center of the design. They were stripped to their waists, like the women in the Sun Dance. The medicine man took handfuls of sand from the painting and rubbed it on them. That was so Dolly would run again, free as the wind. Her father, who was the old man's helper, shook a gourd rattle and sang a slow song that seemed to have neither beginning nor end. Then it was all over and they went out into the courtyard, quietly, as if they were leaving church.

Next day at noon, when the mail was passed out as usual, Mary had a letter from Josephine.

"She's going to get married!" she cried to Jim, tears running down her face. "He's got a job in Poteau teaching, but she wants us to meet him before they decide when. My baby, married!"

"You didn't take on like this when the others got married," Jim snorted.

"But she's my baby! She's the last one!" Mary wept.

Alice came quickly to Jim's rescue. He looked as helpless as any other man in a similar situation, and something had to be done.

"Why don't we all take the day off tomorrow," Alice suggested. "You haven't seen San Francisco yet and it would be too bad to go home for Thanksgiving without doing that. It's only two weeks till we leave, now."

Mary dried her eyes. "They got trading posts there?"

"Big department stores," Alice replied. "You know, like John A. Brown, in Oklahoma City. You could get Josephine a shawl for an engagement present, perhaps."

"I sure like to see that Chinatown," Jim said. "Want to see if those people do look like us."

"Why don't we buy the shawl there?" queried Alice. "They have beautiful ones, with embroidery and fringes—"

"We do that!" Mary exclaimed. "Me and Jim, we've saved all our money since we got here. No place to spend it. We can get her a real nice shawl, and maybe something for Clark, too."

"Good!" Alice agreed.

"Maybe we can see that Pacific Ocean, too," Jim hazarded. "We just see this little piece of it here in the Bay, so far."

"We can do that."

So the next morning they set out. Mary and Jim were waiting when Alice drove over from Berkeley at nine.

"You're early," said Alice.

"We been ready since six," Mary informed her, smoothing down the skirt of her best print dress with a gloved hand. She was dressed as she would be to go to church in Anadarko, as was Jim; Mary wanted to be sure they looked as nice as any people they would meet. And they did.

"We go in the car?" asked Jim.

"I thought maybe we'd leave the car here and go another way," said Alice.

"How?" demanded Mary. Cars were all right, as familiar as horses, but she was a little uncertain about other forms of transportation, except trains.

"You'll see," Alice laughed.

First the "elephant train" (a motor train with the first car made to look like an elephant) from the front of the Federal Building to the ferry slip. The great boat loomed above them, but Mary set her chin and clenched her fists and marched determinedly up the gangplank behind Jim. Alice led the way up narrow stairs to the upper deck. There they could see the whole panorama of the Bay with the city at the end of the bridge, which arched above their heads, raising a tall white tower above the miraculously blue sky. All around the city were the enclosing hills. On this November morning there was no mist, and everything was as clear to their eyes as a toy city.

Mary gasped. "It beautiful!"

The ferry whistle blasted their ears.

"Like a train, but louder," Jim commented. They drew slowly away from the slip, and as the ferry moved across the Bay, the city drew closer and louder, and finally surrounded them as they pulled into the opposite slip, where they could see only the buildings right at hand.

Up Market Street to Powell on a trolley. Then off the trolley to take their places on the open-sided cable car. At Grant Street they got off, and walked into the maze of Chinatown. Mary, entranced with flower stalls, smoked ducks hanging outside meat stores, and dried fish standing in glass jars on open counters, paid little attention to the people.

Jim, on the contrary, watched every face that passed them: little old ladies in long black gowns and soft flat shoes; striding young businessmen and smiling old ones in high-necked blue shirts over loose cotton trousers; young girls, chattering together like birds in vividly colored replicas of their grandmothers' somber gowns. Many of the girls' dresses were split to the knees at the sides and their bare brown legs showed through above their sandaled feet.

"Not very nice," remarked Mary. "They ought to keep their legs covered up like good Indian girls."

There were tea shops and gift shops and dark doorways through which strange food smells emerged into the narrow, crowded street.

Jim wrinkled his nose. "I like to smell beef better," he said.

"Are you getting hungry?" Alice asked.

"Some," said Mary. "We ate a good breakfast, but it was a long time ago."

"We'll buy Josephine's shawl, and then get lunch," Alice decided. "Would you like fish? It's very good in some places here."

"All right," Jim agreed, "I can eat beef at home. Fish is all right."

"Here's the shawl shop," Alice announced, and they went inside.

The shelves were stacked with bolts of many-colored silks, but the shawls were kept under the counter, just as in a trading post. The clerk began to bring them out, one at a time, and spread the rich softness before them.

"Is very expensive?" Mary asked hesitantly.

"Not very," the clerk replied. "Right from China, from capital city, Peking. All hand embroidery. Ten dollars."

Mary let the fringe trickle through her fingers, softer than rainwater and a deep blue. "Real Cheyenne color," she observed.

"Caddos like pink and green," Jim reminded her.

They drew aside, discussing, considering. Ten dollars would buy only half of such a shawl in Anadarko, they well knew. They turned back to the counter.

"We take two," Mary pronounced, speaking very distinctly so

this strange foreign young man should be sure to understand her. "We take this blue one here, and this rose-color one here. Blue and green are the same color, and you know it," she informed Jim, who knew better than to argue on such matters.

"Do you want them wrapped together or separately?" the clerk inquired, being as careful with his English as Mary was with hers.

"Separately," she decided. "They be easier to carry." She could not hold in her pride any longer. "They're for our daughter," she said. "She's got engaged."

"Where do you live?" asked the clerk, busy with paper and silk cord.

"Anadarko, Oklahoma," Jim answered. "We're American Indians. I'm Caddo, and my wife here, she's Cheyenne."

"Are you working at Treasure Island?" the clerk asked.

"Yes. We demonstrate crafts there."

"Many people from the Exposition come here to buy shawls. Very nice people. We feel at home with them."

"They say one time we were all one people," Jim said. "Maybe it's true."

The clerk smiled as he finished tying the packages in red paper. "We say red is lucky for brides," he remarked, and added a red silk rose and a tiny paper parasol under the knot of each package.

They passed a kite shop on the way back to the cable-car stop. Jim stared for moments at the great open-mouthed carp kites soaring above their heads and plunged into the store. When he came out, he held one in his hand.

"For Clark," he said. "All Chinese boys fly kites, the man said."

"Good," Mary agreed. "We take it to him, make him happy, too."

They returned to the cable car's stopping place, and took the next one, up and over the crest of the hill and down the other side to the waterfront. Here they dismounted, while the car was being turned around behind them, and began the walk along the wharf to Joe DiMaggio's Restaurant.

Mary was hungry by now, and would have liked to walk quickly, but Jim's arthritis was bothering him and that slowed them down. There was enough to see here to make you walk slowly, anyway.

The boats were coming in with the morning's catch, and Mary watched, delighted, as a silver stream of anchovies poured down the slide and into the bins on the dock.

"Too little!" she exclaimed. "People eat them little baby fishes?"

Alice laughed. "They're as grown up as they'll ever be," she said. "Yes, people eat them. They're good, too."

There were other bins with larger fish, such as sea bass, red snapper, salmon, trout, and even a few giant salmon, although the season was late for them. Jim was most pleased with the piles of crabs and spiny lobsters sprawled on the boards of the dock, still alive.

"Look!" he instructed Mary. "They're my friends. They're talking to me in sign language.

"Hello, friends," he signed back. "I'm glad to have come to your place. You come to mine sometime. It's pretty dry for you there, though. Maybe we put you in my brother's stock pond."

Mary laughed at him, and drew him on to the bins of scallops and mussels and clams. "Look at all the shells," she said. "I wish I had some of those blue ones. They'd look pretty on the buckskin dress instead of those old white imitation elks' teeth [African cowries] we have to use nowadays when elk's all killed off."

"You'd start a new fashion," Alice observed.

"What's wrong with that? Indians can change. They changed from real elks' teeth to imitation ones when they had to."

"Maybe we can find a shell shop somewhere and buy some."

"That would be good," Mary agreed. "I can take them to the dentist and have him drill holes in them, like he does in the white ones."

They had reached the restaurant and its smell of herbs and wine and salt water by then. Jim looked at it suspiciously.

"Nothing but fish there?" he demanded.

"Oh, they have shellfish, too," Alice replied, and led the way inside and followed the waiter to the table. He put the menus before them.

"What you going to eat?" Mary asked Alice.

"I think I'll have cioppino and a glass of red wine."

"What's cioppino?" Mary inquired.

"It's a kind of fish stew. It has red snapper, and those shellfish you saw, and crab claws. . . ."

"What's crab claws?" Jim asked suspiciously.

"Why, crabs are those things you saw on the dock, waving their claws."

"No!" Jim's face set sternly. "I don't eat my friends. Those things signed to me. And I'm not going to drink any red wine. You can make yourself act silly, but not me."

The waiter had arrived by then, and stood waiting for their orders. Alice looked at Mary, questioningly.

"I eat what you eat," Mary decided, "and I guess I drink a little red wine, too."

"Make you silly," Jim cautioned.

"What do you want?" Alice asked.

"What kind of real fish you got? Not them shelly things."

The waiter ran down the list on the menu. "We have some very nice red snapper today, and I think I can get you some salmon or tuna, and we have sea bass. . . ."

"Bass!" said Jim decidedly. "And coffee," he added. "If I got coffee and these funny sticks of bread, I be all right, but I eat bass, too, like at home."

Even Mary looked a little suspicious when the bowls of steaming hot cioppino arrived and she saw the mussels, still in their shells, and the crab claws, still in their casing, piled on the piece of red snapper and floating in rich gravy.

"How you get them out?" she asked.

Alice showed her how to use the cracker and pick to extract the meat.

Mary's face lit up at the first taste. "It's good!" she cried. "Sweet. Look, Jim, you taste."

"I don't eat my friends," Jim reiterated doggedly. "Caddos aren't Tonkawas. Maybe you got some Tonkawa blood in you?"

Mary carefully accumulated the mussel shells beside her plate, and looked over at Alice's. "I sure like to have those," she remarked wistfully.

Alice added her shells to Mary's, and the pile grew as the meal continued. Contrary to Jim's predictions, the red wine was counteracted by the sea air and the food, with a cup of espresso for dessert, and they did not act silly at all.

Mary wrinkled her nose at the taste of the demitasse. "I guess I drink plain coffee next time," she observed.

Jim shook his head. "You better stick to things you know," he cautioned her. "Maybe all that stuff make you sick."

Alice beckoned to the waiter for the check, and asked him for a bag for the shells. He must have been used to people who took things home, Mary thought, because he provided it without any questions.

"I'll carry the bag," Alice offered. "You have the two fancy parcels, and Mr. Inkanish has his kite. You don't want to get them smelly or greasy."

"You good girl, Ahneece." Mary smiled.

They took the cable car and then the trolley and then the ferry back to Treasure Island. The bus was waiting for them in the courtyard, and the other demonstrators were piling in.

Miss Morrow came over to them. "Did you have a good day?" she asked.

"Like no other day," Mary answered. "I got to think about a lot."

"Sure do," Jim agreed, and they went back to the barracks and straight to bed.

Then began the hustle and stir of closing the show. Little Dolly Lee came back from the hospital, her leg much straighter and stronger, and they all cried joyfully with her mother. Even Mr. Douglas had to blow his nose hard several times. He and Dolly were good friends, and he had missed having her walk around the display area with him when he lectured.

On the very last day, when the late tour group assembled, Mr. Douglas and Mr. d'Harnoncourt were so busy packing paintings that Mr. Douglas forgot about his lecture. The people waited and waited, and Mary watched and wondered if she should send for Alice, who had given the lecture a few times.

Suddenly she saw the group start out, moving from display to display, just at Mr. Douglas' own pace, although he was not with them. Mary went over and slipped into the group. There in front was little Dolly, moving from one display to another and repeating Mr. Douglas' lecture in his own words.

"But she can't speak English!" Mary cried to Miss Morrow, who stood beside her.

"She can hear," Miss Morrow reminded her. "You know yourself that's the way Indian children have always learned, by listening and memorizing."

When the group came out into the show room, and Dolly said "That's all, folks," the way Mr. Douglas always did, everybody laughed and applauded, and some of the people gave her presents of money. She ran to her mother, her full hands outstretched, and was picked up and carried away to the room where they all gathered for tea when it was late afternoon. There was a couch in the room, and Dolly's mother laid her down and patted her to sleep, whispering a little song under her breath.

The trip home did not begin until almost noon the next day. They had to pack and load the car, stowing the precious shawls and kite very carefully.

"We go back the same way?" Jim asked.

"No," Alice answered, "it's too cold in the high mountains now. We'll go back the southern way."

All that afternoon they drove southward, the ocean endlessly to their right, and that night they slept in a motel within sound of the waves. Just before they turned onto the road that led inland, Alice stopped the car and led the way down to the beach. Without speaking, they walked along the sand, and Mary gathered more blue shells as she went along. She had more than enough to trim a dress now.

They were all tired, and they were all in a hurry to get home, for Thanksgiving, for Josephine. The trip back was a blur to Mary. Sometimes she thought Alice was driving too fast, but she did not say so; it meant fewer stops by the way. And then, late on Tuesday evening, they drew up before the house, and Josephine was there, and a tall young man, holding her hand, and Clark running around like an excited colt. Alice kissed Mary and Josephine and said good-bye while the men unloaded the car, and they all watched her drive away to her own family in Oklahoma City.

19

JOSEPHINE GOES

That was a wonderful Thanksgiving. Jim couldn't hide anything as big as Clark's kite, so they had to give it to him right away. He went out into the thin sunshine of the November afternoon, and all the boys in the neighborhood gathered in the front yard to help him fly it.

Mary tried to hold back with the two shawls for Christmas, but late on the night they arrived she could not wait any longer. Besides, there had been no time for Mary to talk alone with Josephine until the family went to sleep, and she wanted to know more about Josephine's young man. All she knew was that he had been introduced as Gerald and he taught at Poteau. She slipped into Josephine's room with the two red-wrapped packages and laid them on the bed.

"For you," she said.

Josephine was sitting at the dressing table with her robe on, brushing her long thick hair. She had cut it once, when she was in high school, but Mary had begged, so she had let it grow back. Now she put down the hairbrush and turned around.

"For me?" she asked.

"For you," Mary repeated.

Josephine sat down on the bed beside her mother, and opened first one and then the other package. The silk poured from its wrappings, even more soft and lustrous than Mary remembered. She picked up the blue shawl, and laid it over the girl's shoulders. "For when you are a Cheyenne Princess," she remarked, and then, when she put the rose-colored shawl around Josephine, "For when you are a Caddo princess."

"I won't be a Princess very long now," Josephine reminded her. "Married women can't be Princesses, you know."

Mary drew a deep breath, and asked the question that had lurked in her mind every mile of the way back from San Francisco. "Who is he? You haven't even told me his full name. All I know is that his name is Gerald. What tribe? How did you meet him?"

"Didn't I tell you?" Josephine exclaimed.

"Just that he's Indian, and you love him and are going to marry him."

Josephine shook her head and laughed at herself. Her fingers began to move, braiding the hair, and she bent her head so as not to look at her mother.

"He's Seneca. He went to that music school up in New York where Augustine Campbell is. When he graduated he decided to teach school for a while and then, when he had enough money saved, go back and take his master's—that's the next highest college degree.

"Well, he has relatives in the Oklahoma Senecas, and he wrote to them, and they found out there was an opening for a music teacher and bandmaster in Poteau, and that the school board really wanted a man, so he applied for it and got it."

"And what is his whole name?"

"Red Leaf. Gerald Red Leaf. That's the name of his Oklahoma relatives, too. They live up near Miami. He plays the clarinet, but oh, Mother, you ought to hear him sing!"

"Church music?"

"Church music, and opera—and oh, just everything. You used to talk about a minister you knew who would sing 'His Eye Is on the Sparrow.' Gerald sings that, just beautifully."

Mary's mind turned back to Seger's Colony School, and the preacher singing that same hymn. She realized, with a start, that the preacher must have been a young man, not much older than this Gerald Red Leaf.

"Did Augustine tell him about you?" she asked.

"She told him about me, and she wrote to me about him. She said I was her sister-friend, and ought to meet him and be nice to him, because he would be a stranger at first. And so we met at the first faculty meeting at Poteau High School this fall, and we've been seeing each other ever since. And then we decided to get married in another two years, when he's saved enough money to go back to Rochester, and we won't have to be apart then."

"What about you? What will you do while he's doing all this studying?"

"Oh, I can get a job teaching in Rochester. I've got a certificate. Remember?"

Mary remembered. Her baby, in the black cap and gown over a white dress last spring, taking the black case which held the diploma from the college president. And now she was grown-up. She was a teacher, and she was going to get married. Mary shook her own thoughts into place inside her head.

Josephine slipped off the rose-colored shawl and put it on her mother. "You take this," she said. "I'll keep the Cheyenne one. You can always use another shawl."

Mary stroked the silk again. "All right," she said. "I'll keep it till you marry and then give it to somebody, maybe Maude, because she's Augustine's mother."

"That's a good idea," Josephine agreed. "Do that." She suddenly, impulsively, kissed her mother's cheek. "Then Maude and Augustine will always have something to remind them of us."

"You keep the roses and the parasols, though." Mary laid them on the bed. "You can put them in your braids when you dance. Look pretty."

"That's a good idea," Josephine said. "I will keep them, because, in a way, they were presents to me."

Mary stood up. "Go to bed now," she ordered. "I go tell your papa."

Jim listened to her account, and nodded solemnly when she had finished. "Better they get married," he agreed. "She's a good pretty girl, and he seems like a nice young man."

"He isn't near good enough for her," Mary sniffed, and turned over on her side, to hide her tears until sleep wiped them away.

But as time came and went, and Josephine and Gerald went back and forth between Poteau and Anadarko in his little open car, they all grew to know him and like him better and better. In the summer Jim found him a job at Riverside Indian school. He lived at the school and he worked outdoors in the school garden. Gerald was a good gardener. Everything seemed to grow well for him.

In the second fall, just before school opened, Josephine came and sat beside Mary on the porch swing in the dusk.

"We want to get married at Christmas," she said softly. "Is that all right with you and Papa? Then we can finish the spring semester and spend the summer here with you before we go to Rochester."

"All right," Mary said. "We want you to be happy, that's all. Just happy."

So when the two young people left for Poteau the next morning, she shook Gerald's hand and said, "Be good to her, that's all. Just take care of her." She turned back and walked, straight and small, into the house, but at the door she turned and waved them away.

Alice was away that year, and so were Mary's other friends, Miss Morrow and Mr. Douglas and Mr. d'Harnoncourt. They were all in New York, where they were putting on another exhibition, this one in a museum. Mary thought of them and missed them. Alice came back in autumn, soon after Josephine left.

"You look tired," Mary informed her. "You too thin."

"We're all tired," Alice agreed. "We worked hard."

"Now what you going to do?"

"I'm going to be at home here in Oklahoma for a while," Alice said, smiling at the thought. "I'm going to set up and open an Indian museum at Fort Sill Indian School."

"Are all the others coming back?"

"Not right away. I'm going to start this one by myself, with some of the people at the school helping me. And I may go out to buy arts and crafts from other tribes for the salesroom."

"You don't got to buy from no other tribes. You can get plenty of arts and crafts right here from us. I take you to good workers."

So once or twice a week Alice drove up from Fort Sill School, and they visited the other members of the Women's Heart Club, and bought beads and hunted for hides, all over again. These were little short trips, an afternoon at a time, but between them Mary and Alice got a lot done.

Early in November Alice said, "I have to go away for a while. I'll be back for Christmas."

"Not Thanksgiving?" Mary demanded. "Josephine's coming home then. You never did really meet that Gerald Red Leaf. You only got introduced to him while we were saying good-bye—when we come back from the Exposition."

"No, and I want to know him," Alice replied. "Maybe I'll meet him at Christmas."

"Yes, you'll meet him then. That's when they're going to get married."

"Find out what kind of present Josephine wants," Alice suggested. "I'd like to bring her something nice."

"Oh, she likes just anything," Mary replied. "Maybe you get her something nice for her kitchen?"

"Good idea," Alice agreed, and got up to go.

Mary looked at her warmly. "Sometimes I feel like you was my daughter, too," she said. "You sure been good to us. You could call me Mama the way Josephine does."

"I'd love to." Alice hugged her and brushed a kiss on her cheek. "Good-bye, Mama. I'll see you at Christmas."

Thanksgiving was gay again this year, and they were all busy with wedding preparations. Josephine and Gerald were to be married in the Presbyterian church, it was decided.

The day the two young people started back to Poteau, the snow began falling softly. Mary worried about Josephine.

"You wrap up warm," she instructed. "You know how easy you catch cold." She brought her own woolen shawl from the closet and swathed Josephine's head and shoulders in it.

Josephine protested. "You need it yourself," she argued, but Mary was firm.

"You wear it," she ordered. "If you go in some place to eat or drink coffee, you can take it off, but put it on again when you go out."

They drove away, with Josephine laughing, and the shawl hiding her head and most of her face.

There was bad news on the radio the next Sunday. Japanese planes had bombed a place called Pearl Harbor, and many people had been killed.

A week later there was worse news. Gerald telephoned. "I guess you'd better come to Talihina"—his voice was sober and tired. "Josephine's in the Indian hospital there. She's real sick."

"How sick?" Mary forced her own voice to be calm.

"She's got pneumonia," Gerald answered. "They don't know yet how bad it is."

If only Alice were there! She would take them, Mama knew. As it was, they had to go by bus. First to Oklahoma City, then a wait and a change and on through Seminole, Wewoka, McAlester. The names went on endlessly. Finally, they were in Poteau.

"I had them get Josephine's room at the boarding house ready for you. You can sleep there, and we'll go to Talihina first thing in the morning," said Gerald.

"Can't we go now?" Mama begged.

"Not till you get some rest. You don't want Josephine to see you looking all tired, do you? That would worry her and make her worse."

Mama sighed, and gave in. Before daylight she was up and dressed, and Jim was ready, too. They followed the smell of coffee to the barren boarding-house dining room. There they drank the coffee without speaking. Jim managed to eat a biscuit, but Mama could not get hers down.

Gerald came in his little car, with Mama's shawl folded on the seat beside him. "It's your turn to wrap up now," he said. "You need it more than Josephine does, for the present."

Mama snuggled into the warm folds, and drew the shawl over her head and tightly around her shoulders. There was no snow here and the weather was warmer than at home, but there was cold inside her, spreading outward from her heart, and she shivered in spite of the warm wrapping.

She hardly saw the blue-misted mountains between Poteau and Talihina. Ouachita, Winding Stair, Talihina—they were all alike with their ups and downs and curving roads. She thought of driving through the mountains of New Mexico and Arizona with Alice, and wished this nightmare mist would go away, letting bright sunlight fall on her again.

At the Indian hospital, the receptionist looked at them. "You're her folks, aren't you? You'd better go right up. She got worse again in the night." She led the way, and they all tiptoed through the long gray corridors on the linoleum-covered floors, where paths had been worn by hurrying feet like their own, so that the brown base showed through.

The nurse opened a door. It was a single room, painted gray like the corridors. On a nightstand beside the bed there were two glasses, one with water and the other with a thermometer.

Josephine lay on her back, her eyes closed. At first Mama thought she was asleep, but when she touched the burning hand that lay on the covers, she recognized the coma that had gripped her uncle at the end. She turned to the nurse. "How long?" she asked.

"Not very long," the nurse replied, and went out softly.

Mary stroked Josephine's hair. Then she sat down on the bed and gathered the girl to her, as she had when Josephine was a baby. Josephine's breath was coming in short, shallow, irregular little gasps. The nurse was right. It would not be long. And it was not. Josephine turned her face against her mother's breast, drew one deep shuddering breath, and then was still. Forever, Mama knew.

The hospital ambulance took them all home, that eighteenth of December 1941. Gerald followed, driving by himself, his face a twisted mask of sorrow. Jim wept openly, as an old man might. He *was* an old man, Mama realized. And she herself, she thought dimly, was an old woman, now that her baby was gone.

Just a week before Christmas, Mama thought. Just a week before they would all have been so happy. Josephine would have worn the new white dress Mama had made for her, and the veil Mrs. Peters said she had worn at her own wedding. She would have been so beautiful. . . .

Josephine wore white before Christmas Day. On the twentieth of December, Mama dressed her in the white buckskin dress for the last time. She wrapped the blue shawl around the girl's shoulders and told the undertaker to put the rose-colored one over the coffin. She laid the drumstick she had snatched from the Sun Dance when she was a child beside her daughter.

"Take it home with you, Mah-hee-yuna," she whispered. "You have truly given yourself for your people." Her face was as calm as Josephine's.

They went again to the sunny hillside, and when the last prayer had been said and Gerald had sung "His Eye Is on the Sparrow" as if

Josephine still could hear the words, Mama took up the rose shawl and handed it to Maude.

"She wanted you to have this," she said, and took Clark's hand and walked away into her own loneliness.

❖◇❖◇❖◇❖◇❖◇❖◇❖◇❖◇❖◇❖◇❖◇❖◇❖◇❖◇❖◇❖◇❖◇❖◇❖◇❖

20

TURNING POINTS

It was not until four days after Josephine's death that Mama thought of the medicine bundle. She unpacked the trunk where it was stored, and sat and looked at it for a long time. Then, very deliberately, she cut the strings and laid the bundle open. One piece at a time, she took out its contents.

After a long time, Mama went out in the yard and cut branches from the cedar trees that flanked the front door.

Jim came out to her, and saw what she was doing. "Why?" he asked.

Mama swung to face him and all her pent-up grief and rage at life burst forth. "That old thing!" she cried. "Nothing but trouble and tears go with it! First my uncle, then my mother, and Sonny, now Josephine—" She choked and stopped. "Now I'm going to burn it, and everything in it. Build me a big fire, Jim. I'm going to burn it, and everything in it."

Jim built the fire on the winter-hard earth of the backyard. Mama brought the bundle, rolled up any which way, out of the house and laid it on the ground, spread open to the sky. One at a time she lifted out its contents, and began laying them in the fire. A stuffed hawk; a bear's paw dried almost beyond identification, so it might have been a man's hand; a buffalo tail; an otterskin, and at the bottom, the little wooden bowl and a horn spoon for mixing medicines, and the bone necklace. Beside the bowl was a straight pipe, a deer's leg bone bound with sinew, and Mama flung it into the flames. But when she picked up the little bowl, scraped with a stone knife from a maple burl, and felt its warmth against her palm;

Frame of the Sun Dance Lodge, with offerings attached to central pole. Men at left are tying a rafter in place.

Preparing the Lone Tipi.

The Lone Tipi.

The Sun Dance Altar, with the Sacred Buffalo Head.

The Sacred Woman, right, and her attendant.

The Sacred Woman, right, being painted, while woman at left prays. Each of the older women has been a Sacred Woman herself.

Head Priest of the Sun Dance, the late Mr. Baldwin Twin, 1961. Partly hidden by tree behind him, a man and boy at prayer.

John Hill, the Sun Dance Camp Crier, or announcer. This was the last Sun Dance Mary attended.

Sun Dance drummers. They are using a regular drum instead of a rawhide slab and shaking rattles made of beef scrotums.

Praying to Maheo.

Food offerings to the dancers.

Sun Dancers touch holy sticks to the sacred fire. Their bodies are painted and they are wearing women's shawls and have willow wreaths on their heads.

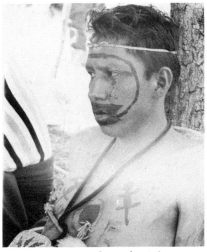

The boy who pledged the Sun Dance to cure his sister, being painted by his sponsor.

A young man, adorned with sacred painting, waiting for the Sun Dance to begin.

Two Sun Dancers with their sponsor.

Bringing food offerings to the dancers.

when she lifted the horn spoon; and when she saw again the necklace her grandmother, her mother, she, and Josephine had worn, she lost heart. Holding them in her hand, she kicked the buffalo-hide wrapping of the bundle into the flames and stood watching, holding her treasures, until it was consumed.

"I keep these," she informed her husband, and he nodded.

Alice came back in January. Her brother was already in military service, in Oklahoma at Fort Sill, where Alice and his young wife had driven him two days before.

"Well, you get to see him sometimes," Mama consoled her.

Alice nodded. "I'll stay at Fort Sill School myself until I finish the job. Then I'm going to work for the Red Cross. There won't be enough money now to pay for museum displays and luxury things like that."

And at the end of June she came to say good-bye.

"Where are the others?" Mama asked fearfully.

"Mr. d'Harnoncourt is working for the State Department. The Army didn't take him."

"Couldn't get a uniform big enough," Papa commented.

"No, it's because he's lived in Mexico and speaks Spanish, and they can use him better there and in South America."

"Where's Dougnas?" she asked, having her usual difficulty in pronouncing the *l* in Douglas' name.

"He's training to be an executive officer in an Army hospital. He doesn't know yet where they'll send him. Probably the Pacific somewhere."

"Pacific is bad." Mama shuddered. "All those young men on that island out there, those the Japanese didn't kill, they captured." She paused a moment. "What about Miss Morow? She go Red Cross, too?"

"No, she's gone to North Carolina, to the Cherokee School, to replace one of the teachers there."

"All gone. All scattered," Mama sighed. "Like leaves come down from cottonwood trees." She shook herself and got up with almost her old briskness. "You wait here," she said.

When she came back, she held the little wooden bowl. "You take it for good-bye," she said, pressing it into Alice's hands. "It would have been Josephine's. Now she's gone and you're our daughter. Keep it safe."

"Hah-hoh!"—"Thank you!" in Cheyenne—was all Alice could say. Then she kissed Mary and Jim and went away, out to her car and her new way of work with the American Red Cross.

Alice did not come back until September 1945, after the war was over and people could take up their lives again. Papa was not well; the doctor said that his arthritis had affected his heart and he must rest a great deal.

Alice put a book in Mama's hands, and Mama sat and looked at it, turning it over and over. *"The Ten Grandmothers,"* she remarked. "The Kiowas got some things called that."

"It's about the Kiowas," said Alice. "Don't you remember, I worked with them before I ever knew you?"

"I remember," Mama sighed, and handed the book to Papa, who studied it in his turn. "No pictures," he observed. "Just them little old scratchy drawings. Books ought to have pictures."

"It cost too much to print them in wartime," was Alice's reply.

"What you going to do now?" Mama asked. "Go back to Arts and Crafts Board?"

"There isn't any more Arts and Crafts Board," Alice informed her. "No, I'm going to New Mexico and start a book about María Martínez. Remember her? The Pueblo lady in San Francisco?"

"Always somebody else," Mama scolded. "When you going to write about Cheyennes?"

"As soon as I can. As soon as we can sit down quietly and put it together. But María's husband, Julian, died the same winter as Josephine, and María isn't getting any younger. I think I'd better do her book first. And I want time to think a little. I'm tired." She looked it.

"You go on, then," Mama instructed her. "When you come back, we start my book."

"That's a promise," Alice said.

She came back in the spring of 1949. Mama saw the car drive up and came out to meet her. Wordlessly, they embraced. Not until they were in the house did Alice ask, "Where's Papa?"

"He's gone," said Mama. "His heart got too tired. He was best man ever I know. We was married fifty years, he never speak cross to me—never to anyone. Everybody love him, me too. Now he's gone."

They sat remembering Chinatown and Treasure Island, and the crabs on the wharf, making signs to talk to Papa. Then Mama smiled.

"We got new arts and crafts museum and salesroom in Anadarko," she told Alice. "Out on highway east of town. Got good man for director—Royal Hassrick. He's friend of Dougnas."

Alice smiled as she watched her struggle with the *r* in the director's name. "Good."

"You take me there, I let you meet him. He's already got wife and chil'rens."

Alice laughed. "He's safe from me, then," she assured Mama, and they went out to the car and drove to the museum.

They were surprised to find Miss Morrow there with Mr. Hassrick. She had come to work with the women on arts and crafts while he got the museum ready to open. They all laughed and talked at once for a few moments; then Mr. Hassrick asked, "Are my moccasins ready?"

Mama drew a cloth-wrapped bundle from beneath her shawl and extended it to him. Inside was a pair of man's moccasins, with a design of antelopes marching around the welt that joined uppers and lowers. Mr. Hassrick pulled off his shoe, and tried one on. He knew how to do it, fitting it from the toes backward, like a glove.

"Beautiful!" he said. "That's a new design to me. We'll call them Inkamocs."

"Is old Cheyenne design," Mama informed him. "Is old design in my family. I like you, Hassnick, so I make them for you." A little smile crinkled the corners of her eyes. "The first pair was the best," she said, remembering. "My mother told me, 'If you going to get married to that man, you got to make him special pair of moccasins.' So I did. Make them all myself. And I put that design, like we make for somebody we going to honor, on them. The last night before we married, I sit up all night, with a lantern, under the wagon, to finish them." She paused.

"Did he wear them to the wedding?" Alice urged.

Mama's eyes and thoughts came back from that time, more than fifty years before. "He couldn't wear them to the wedding, not with his new suit, and store shoes, and all. No, he didn't wear them to the wedding, but in the summer, when the Caddos had the Turkey Dance, we all dress up like old-time Indians. I seen him coming, and I look to see what moccasins he's wearing. Not my moccasins at all! Caddo moccasins! So I say, 'What you do with them moccasins I make you?"

"And he say, 'I'm Caddo. I soak off the beads, and my sister Ahneece, she use them to make these.' Was only time I get mad at him. I say, 'Next time, you let your sister make your moccasins, use her own beads, not mine.' That's all I say. I don't say no more. But I like you, Hassnick, so I make you that design."

"Do you want me to marry you?" Royal Hassrick teased.

"No, I'm too old." Mama was entirely matter-of-fact. "But I like you to be my son, like Ahneece is my daughter."

Royal Hassrick hugged Mama, shook hands with his new sister, and then took them all home with him for lunch.

That was the summer when Mama said to Alice, "I'm getting old, don't see as good any more. I like make trip, go north, and see my people there. See the sacred places."

So that summer, Mr. Douglas said he would pay for the trip if they would take some old beadwork from the Denver Art Museum with them and see what the Northern Cheyennes thought about it. Alice's artist friend, Martha, went with them.

They drove straight north from Denver to Sheridan, Wyoming. Mama told of how there came to be two Cheyenne groups; how they all once were moved out of Montana to Oklahoma. Some of them could not stand the heat and the dust and ran away, back to the clear water and the tall pines of their own old north country. There they had stayed, although members of the two groups still visited back and forth.

It was Sun Dance time when they reached the Agency at Lame Deer, and the Cheyenne camps were clustered at Busby, twenty miles away. For the four public days of the Sun Dance they drove back and forth between Lame Deer and Busby to watch.

The people in the camps fed them, and honored them as guests. They gave Mama a shawl from the trading post, and the two younger women sheets and pillow cases, for these people had no crafts; they had forgotten them, until Mama showed them the old things from the Denver Museum, and how to make them. She was busy, and very happy—happier than she had been in years.

"You been to three Sun Dances," she remarked to Alice one morning at breakfast. "You got to go to four before you can be a real Cheyenne. Crows are having theirs at Crow Agency next week. We go."

"Did you know about it?" Martha asked Alice.

"No, I hadn't heard."

"Then how does she know?"

"How do you know?" she pressed Mama. Mama shook her head.

"Indians knows," she said.

"Didn't you ever hear of the moccasin telegraph?" Alice laughed.

"I've heard of it, but I never believed it before," said Martha. She went out to put the camp stools they had bought in Lame Deer into the car.

At the Crow Sun Dance a wonderful thing happened. It was late on the afternoon of the fourth day, and the dancers all were tired, but they were still dancing.

The Sun Dance priest stood up suddenly—a tall old man, towering over the buffalo-skull altar the Crows used. He put his whistle in his mouth and walked, blowing it steadily, to the center pole. There, while everyone's eyes were on him, he put the end of the whistle against the bare wood of the pole and sucked four times, as if he were a medicine man curing someone ill.

When he drew the whistle away from the pole, a stream of water gushed out, splashing on the ground and making little puddles of mud. They all saw it. "I never see like that before!" Mama exclaimed, and she threw back her head and gave the victory cry.

The Crow people all stared at her, and then one woman went to her tent and brought back a pair of new moccasins, beaded with flower designs. She handed them to Mama. "Got no horses no more," she said. "These the best we got. Is big day, when Cheyenne cheer for Crow."

Other women brought Mama presents, and one gave Martha and Alice each a silk handkerchief, tied around a softly aromatic powder. "Indian love medicine," she said. "Now maybe you each get yourself a man."

Mama put her hand on Alice's shoulder. "This one my daughter," she informed the woman. "She don't need no Crow man. She give her life for the Indians." Nothing more was said then.

Instead of going directly back to Denver, they decided to take a long loop around, through the Arapaho country, to Yellowstone. Before they left, one day when Martha was finishing a painting of the hills behind Lame Deer, Mama and one of her cousins took Alice to see one of the sacred places where Cheyenne men went in the old days for power and blessing. It was a bare, reddish sandstone butte, standing stark above the plain.

"You look up the side," Mama instructed. "One time there was a Cheyenne woman out gathering wild potatoes with her little girl. They going along all right when they hear something behind them, and look around. 'Might be something bad,' the mother say. Sure enough, it was a bear.

"She drop her wild potatoes, and they spill all over everywhere. Then she grab her little girl's hand, and start running, while the bear eating those potatoes up.

"They run fast, and see a little hill ahead of them. Just a little hill, but maybe it be enough to stop that old bear. So they run, run, up the side of the hill, and the hill start to grow, up to the sky, while they still running. And the bear run after them, but the hill keep growing and the woman and her little girl keep running, and finally that old bear give up.

"If you live right, and your heart is good, you will get a blessing here. You will see that woman's tracks, that little girl's tracks, 'bout halfway up, and if Maheo wants to, he will give you a present. But first you got to give him a present."

"I don't think I'm good enough," Alice protested. "Besides, I'm not a Cheyenne."

"You more Cheyenne than these young peoples we got now," the cousin said. "You give Maheo tobacco. That prove it."

Silently, Alice took four cigarettes from her case, and crumbled them on the ground at the foot of the butte.

"Now, look up," Mama directed.

Alice looked up. There, at the top of the butte and leading over its edge, were the footprints of a woman and a child. Perhaps they were petroglyphs, pecked in the rock long ago. Perhaps they were natural formations, and the light struck them in such a way as to make them look like footprints. Alice never knew. But she nodded, and said in a hushed voice, "I see them."

"Now look down," Mama ordered. Alice peered at the ground at her feet. At last she saw it: a large white trade bead, so old that the gloss had worn off its surface glass and it looked like a white pebble. But when she picked it up, the hole through it was unmistakable. Not the hourglass drilling of an Indian bow-drill, but the straight piercing of a European glassmaker.

"Thank you, Maheo," she breathed, and held it tightly.

"Put it in your perfume handkerchief," Mama instructed, "and you be all Cheyenne."

"It's Crow perfume," Alice objected.

"No difference," Mama reassured her. "We all use same plants to make perfume."

Alice drew out the silk handkerchief that she had stuffed in her bra, and dropped the bead into it.

"Keep it there till some man gives you something to go with it," said Mama. "Then you have all kinds of power."

They left for Yellowstone National Park the next day. On their way they drove through the Northern Arapaho reservation. The Arapahoes had not run away from Oklahoma; some of them simply hid in the rocks and refused to go there in the first place.

They saw the Shoshonis, who were silent people, not like the Arapahoes or Cheyennes. And at last they came to the town of Cody, the gateway to Yellowstone National Park.

It was late, so they spent the night in town and telephoned for a cabin in the park for the next two nights. In the morning Mama got the others up early. Her clothes were all packed in her little tin suitcase. "We go now," she said. "This is a sacred place."

It was with some difficulty that Alice persuaded her to eat some breakfast, and as soon as the meal was finished they set out, up the road and to the Ranger station at the park entrance.

"Keep your windows rolled up," said the Ranger as he stuck a pass on the windshield in front of Martha.

"We'll smother!" Martha protested.

"Would you rather smother or shake hands with them, lady?" the Ranger inquired, gesturing toward the brown bears that were crowding around the cars and even scrambling over some of them, begging for handouts.

"I'll smother!" Martha decided.

But Mama cried out, "Is true! The old people all say so! Bear is our ancestors, and we all come from here. We split up one time and Maheo let the bears stay here like always, but he turn the Cheyennes into people and drive them out."

"I've heard other Indians say that," the Ranger said.

With closed windows, they drove on to the Paint Pots, bubbling springs of different-colored mud. There were no bears in sight.

"Stop the car," Mama directed. "This where we used to get that blue paint for trimming moccasins." From nowhere she produced a jar and a spoon, climbed out of the car, and before either of the other women could stop her was out on the quaking sand scooping up blue mud, until she could return, satisfied, with a jarful.

They saw many other wonders that day. That night, when they had returned to the cabin, they saw the full moon just beginning to crest over the eastern mountains. Then they fell asleep.

Alice was wakened by a wild cry.

"Ahneece! Ahneece! The ancestors know we are here, and they come to make a feast!"

It was true: In the moonlight they plainly saw the ubiquitous Yellowstone bears systematically overturning garbage cans and going through their contents for tidbits.

"Don't go out, Ahneece!" Mama cried, although Alice had no intention of doing anything of the sort. "They steal you to marry you. You all Cheyenne now."

Martha left them in Denver, to fly east to her family and her studio, but Mama and Alice stayed on for a few days. They worked with Mr. Douglas, sorting and identifying the Cheyenne material in the museum collection.

It was during this time that Mama caught Alice's hand as she reached for a piece of beadwork. "Your skin's all funny," she observed.

"Oh, I always freckle in the summer," Alice answered casually. "It goes with red hair."

"That not freckles," Mama contradicted her. "That's not good; freckles is all right. Does it itch?"

"Oh, sometimes it burns."

"You didn't have it when we went to Montana."

"It didn't show then because I hadn't been out in the sun."

Mr. Douglas turned from his note taking and looked at Alice's arms and neck. "It's called vitiligo," he said, "and Mama's right. It is a disease; the melanin is burning out of the skin. You just have to tough it out. Sometimes it bleaches out entirely."

"You been touching eagle feathers?" Mama demanded abruptly. Alice waved her hand around the workroom where they sat. There were eagle feathers everywhere: in war bonnets, fans, dance costumes, trimmings on shirts.

"How can I do this kind of work without touching them?" Alice countered.

"I don't mean these old dead things," Mama snapped, "I mean a live feather from a live bird. Did you ever?"

"Why, yes, once," Alice said slowly, remembering. "When I went away to the Red Cross, Dorothy Kawaykula had a dance for me—the Apache Young Woman's Dance. At the end, she put a feather from a live eagle in my hair for a blessing."

"Have you still got it?" Mr. Douglas demanded instantly. "If we had it—and the documentation—it would be a good thing for the collection."

"Eric," Alice said, "I will do practically anything for you and add practically anything I have to the collection, but there are some things I want to keep. You conned me out of the finest set of men's silver hair plates I ever saw. . . ."

"You both silly," Mama announced loftily. "You said we go back by New Mexico, Ahneece. I fix you then, when we get where there's native cedar. Then I clean you up."

The next day, before they left, Mr. Douglas gave them each a present to remember the summer by. To Mama he gave a pair of silver bracelets, set with small even turquoise oblongs all around the band.

"I wear it always, Dougnas," she said, and embraced him.

Alice's gift was a little turquoise bear, carved at Zuñi Pueblo, to keep her white bead company, and a silver-link charm bracelet so she could wear them where they would show.

"Now she never get a man, Dougnas," Mama informed him. "You fix her so she have to give to the Indians, always."

There was much to see and do when they reached Santa Fe. They went to San Ildefonso Pueblo first, to visit María Martinez, and the two old ladies talked long and earnestly about the younger woman they both called "daughter."

Then Alice said, "Now we'll go to Nambe Pueblo, and visit my friends there."

"There are witches in that place," María remarked thoughtfully. "Maybe it's not safe to take your mother there, Alice."

"It's always been safe for me," Alice protested. "She's a good woman. Nothing will hurt her."

"Who are you going to see?"

"Grandmother Leonidas Vigil."

"That's all right. She's a white witch. You'll be safe when you're with her."

"What's a witch?" Mama inquired as they drove along the valley beside a little stream.

"A black witch is a person who does mischief, who hurts people. A white witch does good, and fights the black witches."

"And this woman we go to see—she's a white witch?"

"Yes. She's more than that. She's what they call a *curandera;* she makes sick children well."

"Maybe she help me with you," Mama said, and was silent as they drove through the cold grayness of old Nambe Pueblo, with its great circular *kiva* towering over them, and across the fields and through the orchards beyond it. The trees were heavy with fruit that year, but the native junipers grew in the pastures, many of them already showing the smooth green of the mistletoe that would be coral-colored by Christmas time.

"That's good," said Mama. "Lots of cedar here. Lots blue berries already on those trees."

Grandmother Leonidas welcomed them to her old adobe house. "Come in," she said, shaking hands.

Mama stepped over the high doorsill and down into the plain whitewashed room.

"Why you make the door that way?" she inquired.

"To keep out the burros and chickens. In the old days, when this house was built, by my mother's grandmother's grandfather, they didn't have pens for the animals and the chickens. Just the turkeys."

"Ask her if she got turkey feathers, Ahneece," Mama whispered.

Alice repeated the question.

"Sure I got turkey feathers. You want wild or tame?"

"You got wild turkey feathers?" Mama was really excited now.

"Why you want them?"

"Show her your arms, Ahneece."

Grandmother Leonidas studied the skin blotches a long time. "We know that sickness. You know how to cure it?"

Mama nodded importantly. "Sure I know. It come from a woman handling live eagle feathers. No Cheyenne woman can touch those things."

"Can I watch?" said Grandmother Leonidas. "My nephew has that sickness."

"Yes, you can watch," Mama agreed. "We come back in the morning, and we fix her." Slowly she took from her handbag four one-dollar bills and laid them before Grandmother Leonidas. "You help me, give me wild turkey feather, and we make her well. We be here by sunrise."

"You better sleep here," Grandmother Leonidas said, gathering up the money. "Then we be sure we all together on time."

After supper, as the sun set, the two women gathered juniper. They sent Leonidas' grandsons scurrying around to bring in more and more branches. Before it was quite dark, they had built a little hut for the fragrant wood, and piled more wood in the center of its floor to make a fire. Mama stripped off all the blue juniper berries she could gather, and set them to soak in a cup of fresh water from the river.

In the morning, as the sky was paling, they went outdoors and faced east. Each of the older women prayed softly, mumblingly, in her own language. They wore no clothing, but were wrapped in old soft blankets. As the sun reached the rim of the world, Mama led Alice into the hut and lighted the fire.

She bathed Alice in the fragrant smoke, and when the fire had died and there were only ashes left, she rubbed them all over Alice's body. She reached out through the little door of the hut.

"Give me the cup," she said to Leonidas, and then she held it out to Alice. "Drink it all," Mama commanded. "Every bit."

"Berries and all?"

"Berries and all. You think they poison or something? I don't poison you."

Alice obeyed. The juniper tea was bitter, but she forced it down.

"Now you go down to that creek behind the house and bathe," said Mama. "Wash yourself good, all over." She turned to Leonidas. "That's all there is to it," she said. "Just the prayers—I teach them to you in Cheyenne, if you want—and the smoke and the ashes and tea, and then the bath. Look, she's throwing up. That means we got it all out of her."

And for some reason, or for all, and for the love both women had shown her, within a year Alice's fair skin was bleached white and fair again, with no more ugly brown blotches.

When they reached Anadarko, and the car was unloaded, Mama drew Alice close to her.

"You good girl," she whispered. "Now I been everywhere, seen everything I want to see. Now I sell this big house and buy me little one near the museum, and make moccasins. Pivé! Hah-hoh!" (It is good. Thank you.)

21

✧◇✧◇✧◇✧◇✧◇✧◇✧◇✧◇✧◇✧◇✧◇✧◇✧◇✧◇✧◇✧◇✧◇✧◇✧

NEW FACES, NEW NAMES

Eric Douglas died, of cancer, in the spring of 1956. Everyone mourned him deeply, each in her own manner. Mama wept aloud, wailing as Alice had never heard her before. "He was more than a son to me," she wept. "He was a brother."

Alice could only be glad the long struggle was over. Her grief was that she should have lost a friend and guide. She was purely selfish, and said so.

"No, Ahneece. He is gone. We shall never have another friend like him."

"Not just like him," Alice agreed, "but we will always have friends. You know that. It will happen."

And it did. That summer Carol came from New York to begin research with the Sac and Fox Indians near Shawnee.

"What she want to waste her time with them old people for?" Mama sniffed. "Nice girl like her, she be better off studying Cheyennes. She learn more. I tell you what, Ahneece. We take her to Sun Dance. Then she learn quick. Now all she does is powwow around."

So Carol was invited to go with them to the Sun Dance, and accepted. On the appointed day, she and Alice drove to Anadarko. Mama came out with her shawl, the little tin suitcase she always carried, and a wide sun hat.

"We go to El Reno," she informed them.

"I thought the Sun Dance was at Watonga," Alice protested.

"It is. El Reno's on the way."

"Well, you can get from El Reno to Watonga, all right," Alice

202 / *Dance Around the Sun*

agreed, "but it's about like going to Muskogee by way of Lawton."

"We go to El Reno." Mama was adamant. "We pick up my cousin, Minnie Big Bear, all go to Sun Dance."

"I didn't know you had a cousin named Minnie," said Alice, sighing over a genealogy to be redone yet again. "I thought Minnie was your friend, Minnie Cross, at Colony."

"She's my friend," Mama said impatiently, "but this my cousin, my mother's aunt's daughter. Sometimes they call her Minnie Good Bear. Means the same thing in Cheyenne. Good, Big, they all the same."

Alice argued no more. She backed the car out of the driveway and drove toward El Reno.

"Where does Minnie live?" Carol asked when they reached the outskirts of the town.

"In Clinton."

"But you said El Reno," Alice cried.

"She don't live here. She's visiting her daughter."

Following a series of rather complicated instructions, Alice eventually reached a small white house on the east side of town. Mama, slowly, agedly, got out of the car, went up the walk, and knocked on the door. Another woman, about Mama's age, came out and they embraced. Then they all collected Minnie's suitcase, her shawl, an extra blanket in case the 100-degree temperature turned cold, and the "spit can" that went with her chewing tobacco, and started out again.

"Where we going to stay in Watonga?" Mama asked.

"I thought maybe Roman Nose Lodge would be nice," Alice said. "The park's pretty and there's plenty of shade. We could have a picnic down by the creek. There are lots of tables."

"Not nice," Minnie was positive. "My granddaughter go there one time on high school class party. She say bedbugs in rooms and she come home with nits in her hair."

"It's a state park," Alice argued. "It ought to be all right."

"You see," said Minnie direly. From then on, conversation in the back seat was confined to Cheyenne, while the two in the front seat discussed the coming Sun Dance in English.

They stopped at the Lodge, which looked clean enough. Alice went in, and returned with a key in her hand.

"I got a double cabin," she remarked. "Then we can all be together."

"You pay them any money?" Mama demanded.

"Yes, I paid the deposit. It's down this drive a little way."

"You don't get your money back, I bet," snorted Minnie.

The door of the cabin was ajar. It hung askew on one hinge. The beds were unmade, and soiled blankets trailed on the floor. There was not even a curtain over the bathroom doorway.

"You see," Minnie reminded her. "Not nice."

"Well, we certainly can't stay here," Alice agreed. Key in hand, she drove back to the Lodge. When she emerged from it, she was smiling, and she held up a fan of bills, to show them that she had, too, got her money back. Without another word, they drove on into Watonga.

"Let's get lunch," Carol suggested, and Alice meekly inquired, "Where's the best place, Mama?"

"That cafe on Main Street. White Star, they call it."

The food at the White Star Cafe was what food at a White Star Cafe usually is. They ordered chicken-fried steak, mashed potatoes, canned corn, bread and butter, and coffee.

"Didn't anybody in Oklahoma ever hear of green beans?" Carol asked.

"They grow them in their gardens, but you wouldn't eat them," Alice observed.

"Why not?"

"They'd be cooked with salt pork, for hours, until you couldn't recognize them."

"Oh."

"What you girls so fussy about?" Minnie asked. "This good food, lots of it." She turned to Mama. "You don't teach her so good; she too fussy. They both your daughters?"

"No, just the red-haired one."

"Then I take the other as my granddaughter, bring her up right," Minnie decided. "You got Indian name?" she asked Carol.

"The Sac and Fox Indians in Oklahoma call me *Musquaki-Ikwayah.* That means 'Woman of the Fox Tribe' because I used to work with the Sac and Fox Indians in Iowa."

"You give me tobacco, I give you a name." Then Carol produced the ritual four cigarettes, and passed them across the table.

"I name you 'Laughing Woman,' because you all the time laughing, making jokes," she told Carol. "What's her Cheyenne name?"—she jerked her chin at Alice.

"I haven't given her one yet," Mama answered.

"I beat you!" Carol crowed. "I got my Cheyenne name first!"

There was not only the White Star Cafe in Watonga, there was also a White Star Motel, and it was there they decided to stay. Minnie had another daughter in the town, and preferred staying with her, so Mama luxuriated in a room of her own, adjoining the double room Carol and Alice occupied.

"Now we go buy groceries," she anounced when the car was unloaded.

"But we just ate," Carol exclaimed.

"We buy groceries for Sun Dance camp. Got lots friends there. Got to take presents."

And groceries they bought: sugar, coffee, bread, meat (Alice refused to buy ground beef, hot dogs, or lunch meat in that heat, but got a slab of "boiling beef" and had it cut in four pieces so they could have gifts for four camps), canned tomatoes, canned peaches, and packaged cookies. When all was loaded to Mama's satisfaction, they drove to the open field, overlooking the town, where the lodge frame was being completed.

"They have special dance tomorrow morning," Mama said, with a little contented sigh.

"Oh, look!" Carol exclaimed. "What a beautiful little spaniel puppy. I wonder whose he is. He hasn't got a collar or tags, or anything. Let's take him till we can find his owner, anyway."

"We can't do that," Alice said. "We can't just go around picking up other people's dogs."

"You want him, you take him now," Mama remarked. The puppy had come over, and tail wagging briskly, was licking Carol's extended fingertips. "Better you take him if you want him," Mama reiterated.

But no arguments prevailed over Alice's conscience, and they left the puppy, still wagging his tail, and went to Mrs. Daylight's camp, where they were welcomed warmly, especially when the first sack of groceries was produced.

"She just got name"—Mama pointed her lips at Carol. More and more she was using the gestures of her girlhood; more and more often she used sign language instead of the English words that came harder to her than the Cheyenne she thought she had forgotten. "We got to give presents, show our respect for her."

"What name?" asked Mrs. Daylight.

"Laughing Woman, Minnie called her."

"Pretty name," commented Mrs. Daylight. "She be happy all times with that name."

From camp to camp they went, and each time Carol was introduced by her new name. People shook hands with her, and thanked her for their presents, and everyone agreed she had a pretty name.

"May I take pictures?" she asked Mama when they returned to the motel.

"Not here," said Mama. "Not this Sun Dance. These not my band people. Next year we go to Seiling, to Sam Buffalo's place. You take them there. That be better Sun Dance, and he's my band."

"All right," Carol agreed. She turned to Alice. "I didn't know I would be here next summer."

"Well, I guess you will be," Alice informed her. "Mama sounds pretty definite."

Back at the camp next morning, they looked again for the puppy, but he was not to be seen amid the confusion of the Dance.

They ate noon dinner at Mrs. Daylight's camp, and she was particularly insistent that they share one pot of stew.

"That's not beef, that's a blessing," she insisted.

The meat was mild and light in flavor, and they each ate a little, then filled up with fresh melon they had bought at a roadside stand.

All afternoon they sat out in the hot sun and watched the Dance. The field was on a high bluff that overlooked the town to the south. Dark clouds filled with rain were moving closer and closer. Everyone prayed that the Dance would end before the rain came and lessened the blessing to the dancers. Still closer and closer the clouds came. You could see the rain falling in town, and then the clouds moved toward the Sun Dance. It was almost the end of the Dance and the dancers were getting ready to run out of the Lodge in the four directions. The clouds were now at the foot of the bluff, and as if by magic Maheo stopped them until the dance had ended. And then the rain fell.

That evening back at the motel Carol said, "I wish I knew what happened to that puppy."

"Maybe he got home," said Alice, consolingly.

"That puppy—he got home, all right," said Mama. "We ate him."

Carol paled and Alice choked, thinking of their noon meal, but it was too late to do anything now. They had eaten a share of the puppy; they had received Maheo's blessing, for Maheo gave the Cheyennes the dog sacrament, and to protest or object would be rudeness of the worst kind. So they went to bed, all of them.

After the Sun Dance they returned to Anadarko and deposited Mama. Minnie stayed in Watonga with her daughter, and Carol and Alice went back to Oklahoma City.

"You hear an awful lot in anthropology these days about the nonparticipant observer," Carol remarked on the way home, "but I'd say we participated fully."

"We certainly did," Alice agreed. In her heart she wondered if Mama had known what would become of the puppy, and decided that she had, all along.

The next to come to Anadarko to visit Mama that summer was Father Powell, from Chicago. With him came John Stands In Timber, whom Mama and Alice had met briefly during their Montana summer; he was a Mennonite preacher as well as a Sun Dance priest. Of course he remembered Mama and wanted to see her, so Carol took a day off from studying Sac and Fox weaving, and they all four journeyed to Anadarko.

"You come too late," Mama scolded John. "You miss good Sun Dance."

"Maybe next year," Father Powell consoled her. "I'd like to see it down here."

"Is different from north country," Mama agreed. "Next year, the mens make their ceremony first four days; women stay in camp and be quiet. They let you in, though."

"What kind of preacher are you, anyway?" she asked Father Powell, looking at the black suit and the clerical collar. "Them's hot clothes, for this weather."

"Anglican," Father Powell told her. "What some people call Episcopalian."

"We used to have that kind come to preach at Colony School," Mama murmured. "Joshua Givvens, he come."

"I've heard of him," answered Father Powell. "He was Kiowa."

"Kiowa," Mama repeated. Her mind could see the short, thin young man, in his high-standing collar and pressed white man's clothes, standing before the rows of subdued children, a black book in his hand. "He always read the prayers, not just say them with his heart, like some."

"I always read them," said Father Powell. "I might make a mistake if I didn't."

"Well, we all go to Sun Dance next year," Mama decided. "You be here for Colony powwow, Labor Day?" she asked John.

"Be back home by then," John said. "Father and me got to get back to work."

"Too bad," Mama said, "I need two friends then."

"You have lots of friends, and we'll be there with you," Alice assured her.

Father Powell was interested in Cheyenne religion, and he and Mama and John talked all morning about the Great Race and the White Buffalo Woman.

"You girls go on into town now," Mama ordered finally. "I going to talk about something I don't want you to hear." Obediently, they rose. "You go to the store, get meat, Ahneece," Mama instructed. "Too hard for me to carry much these days, and we got to make feast for our friends from the north country."

On the way out, Alice checked the kitchen cupboards and the refrigerator. They were almost bare. She and Carol went to a chain grocery store and stocked them with meat, frozen vegetables, several loaves of bread and frozen biscuits, canned and fresh fruit, milk, oatmeal (for which Mama had lately developed a taste), and canned soups, tea, and coffee. At the last minute Carol provided a cake.

The door of the front room was closed, and they could hear Mama talking softly behind it when they returned. They cooked hamburgers, and laid out a picnic meal, before the door opened and the others joined them in the kitchen. The canned peaches were opened and set out in a bowl. Coffee perked on the stove, and mustard, mayonnaise, pickles, and catsup were set out, with paper plates and napkins. There was another bowl of sliced fresh tomatoes, onions, and cucumbers. The picnic feast was ready, with Carol's pink cake towering over all the rest.

"You good girls—real daughters," Mama said, and embraced them both. "You say Grace," she instructed Father Powell. "Preacher always got to say Grace."

"I wish my Grandma Minnie could be here," Carol said.

"Maybe she come next time. Sure to be at Colony, with Minnie Cross, if she feels well enough. But I still need two men friends there," Mama insisted.

When they left at the end of the afternoon, she gave each man a pair of moccasins. "Women's sizes," she said. "You got wife?" she queried Father Powell.

He laughed. "A wife, two daughters, and two sons."

"Maybe one of them can wear these," Mama said. Alice knew she had planned to sell them at the museum, and what the money would have meant, and thought gratefully of the kitchen, stocked again. From the corner of her eye she saw Father Powell slip a bill under Josephine's picture, standing in its frame on the table.

Mama would not tell them why Colony powwow became so important in her mind. She only said that she thought the two Minnies—Minnie Cross and Minnie Big Bear—would be there, and that her old friend John Fletcher and his son-in-law were coming, too.

"John bring his white wife, maybe," Mama said, "but you ought to have another friend besides Carol, Ahneece."

So Alice asked her friend, Mary Stith, Editor of the University of Oklahoma Press, and Mary said that she would come. They all stayed at a motel in Weatherford, and drove back and forth the twelve miles to Colony. Mama declined Minnie Cross's invitation to stay with her. She had come to prefer the air-conditioned comfort of a motel room on the various trips.

The first three days of Colony powwow were beautiful, with just a little cool in the air to make it comfortable. They visited Minnie Cross in her little house, and their other friends in the camps. Everybody fed them; everybody talked to them; and it was a happy, friendly time.

Mama and John Fletcher spent hours sitting on a log, talking, talking. Sometimes they sent for John's son-in-law, Willie Hale, and used him as a messenger to one of the hereditary chiefs. It was all mysterious and secret, but Mama was in command of the situation, and she held the reins tightly.

There were dances and give-aways in the afternoons, and social dancing at night. Shawl fringes swung and dyed feathers shone as the dancers moved in the circling, inward-facing line of the round dance, around and around the drum, or became the spokes of a wheel with the drum as its hub in the war dance.

On Saturday morning, before they left Weatherford for Colony, Mama took Alice and Carol and Mary Stith to the department store. There they purchased sheets, pillowcases, and towels, enough for four families. Mary wanted to help with the buying but Mama sternly refused to let her. Only Alice and Carol could spend their money. She took the packages back to the motel, and stowed them safely away.

Sunday morning was hot and cloudy and oppressive.

"Storm building up," Mama observed. "Hope it holds off till evening."

The camps were quiet, but with a feeling of tension from the dense heat of the air. After noon dinner, about two o'clock, dark piles of clouds began forming in the northwest. Mama and John Fletcher held a conference with the announcer, and he began calling the people to the dance ring. When they had assembled he announced, "A special for Mary Inkanish."

Mama put Carol on her left and Alice on her right, and the three circled the dance ring, behind John Fletcher and Willie Hale. When they returned to the speaker's stand, John Fletcher took up the microphone.

"I am speaking for my friend, Vee-hay-kah," he began. "She wishes to honor these two as her friends, and to give them Cheyenne names." He paused, bent forward, and whispered to Mama. "This little one she names Laughing Woman, the name her Cheyenne Grandmother, Minnie Big Bear, has already given her." He shook hands solemnly with Carol. "Because Minnie is sick and isn't here today, Mary takes her as her granddaughter, too." Mama embraced Carol, and handed her one pile of linen. As John called their names, two women came forward, and Carol divided the pile equally between them."

"Now this other one," John went on. "We've all known her for a long time. First we honor her friend from Norman, Mary Stith." Mama put a necklace with a medallion on it around Mary's neck, and thrust a pair of beaded combs into her fair hair.

"Now we give this one a name," continued John. "Her name is Spirit Woman, Mah-hee-yuna, because she has given her life for the Indian people." This time he called Minnie Cross and Sophie Rhodes, Minnie Big Bear's daughter, and Alice gave the presents to them. Mama gave Alice a hawk-feather fan, and they all danced solemnly around the drum again.

It had been growing steadily darker and more threatening while the naming ceremony went on, and just as they returned to the speaker's stand, a bolt of lightning struck the hillside to the north of them and thunder crashed. Great raindrops fell, and everyone scrambled to shelter.

"Perhaps Maheo is angry about my name," Alice gasped as she tumbled in behind the wheel of the car.

"No," said Mama. "He is glad the name goes on. Thunder is the great red horse he rides for victory. He's glad. You'll see."

And as they reached the highway the sky cleared and the storm ended as suddenly as it had begun.

"He's blessing us," Mama said. "We'll be all right now. The name goes on."

22

THE LAST SUN DANCE

Mama grew increasingly frail that winter. She still kept house, cooked, and made some beadwork, but she tired easily.

A new Director, Laurance Cone, whom Mama called Mr. Cones, had taken Royal Hassrick's place at the museum, and when Mama went anywhere but to the grocery store, Joe driving her in his taxi, she would stop off at the museum office to sit and talk with Mr. Cone. Then he would drive her home and drink coffee with her, and they would talk some more.

"You like him, don't you?" Alice asked on one of the visits she and Carol made more frequently now.

"I like him," Mama agreed. "Maybe we take him to Sun Dance this summer. That's all he talks about—Sun Dance. Bad as Father Powell."

"Father Powell and John Stands In Timber will be here for Sun Dance this summer. I just got a letter," Alice informed her.

That year, 1961, the Sun Dance was held at Seiling, northwest of Anadarko. The three women and Mr. Cone drove up on Thursday, and Mama's face lighted with a smile when she saw Father Powell and John waiting for them.

Greetings were exchanged, luggage unloaded and carried into the shiny new motel, and there was excited talk before they went downtown to Brownie's Cafe. After supper, the men went on to the field where the lodge and the Lone Tipi already stood.

The next morning, Friday, they all went to the Sun Dance camp.

"Good thing we don't come yesterday," Mama observed, looking at the ring of tents around the lodge. "Just have to sit in camp and be quiet all day. We got enough men to go round this time. I take John, 'cause he's old like me. Carol, you take Father, 'cause he's little, like you. Ahneece, that leaves you with Mr. Cones."

"Delighted," Laurance murmured, and they all bowed solemnly to each other.

"Ralph White Tail is going to give me a name," said Father Powell. "They said Sunday, at sunrise. Will you all come?"

"Sunrise?" Mama demanded. "I don't know. Sun come up pretty early these days."

"The rest of us will," Carol agreed. "I never really saw the naming ceremony at Colony—I was in it. What's your name going to be?"

"I don't know yet," Father Powell replied. "They said it was the name of a big chief, a long time ago. He was an Arrow priest besides being a chief, so they thought it would be appropriate for me."

"Must be Two Moon," Mama reflected. "Well, you tell me when you know it. We go to my cousin's camp now. Maybe she got fry bread and something else good to eat."

Carol and Alice exchanged glances. One thought was in both heads. The last time they had something good to eat . . .

"I won't eat it if I don't recognize it," Carol said with determination.

Fortunately they were offered unmistakable beef stew and coffee with the fry bread, which was made in the shape of turtles. "My clan, we got the right to make it that way at Sun Dance. You get a blessing from it," Mama told them, when they exclaimed over it. "No other time; just Sun Dance. Come on. We eat; now we go to Sun Dance lodge."

When they got there, the paints on the dancers' bodies were being washed off by the sponsors, and women were bringing in tubs and kettles of food. Visitors were called into the lodge to receive their gifts, and Mama rejoiced over an enormous bowl of rice and raisins.

"Enough for all of us," she announced. "We eat it right up now, while it's hot, so it don't spoil." And full of beef stew and fry bread as they were, they meekly obeyed her instructions.

Mary, with moccasins, about 1962.

Mary, left, with grandson Clark and unknown visitor.

Mary's son Joe, Clark's father.

Mary showing old Cheyenne beaded legging from Denver Art Museum to North Cheyenne men, whose people had lost this craft. At left, Alice Marriott.

*Mary, with Royal B. Hassrick, director of the
Southern Plains Museum, Anadarko.*

*Mary, far right, and Hassrick's successor, L. James Schaeffer, second
from left, with friends, at the Southern Plains Museum.*

Mary, left, and her cousin,
Minnie Good Bear.

Mary, at her last Sun Dance.

Feeding the guests at the Colony powwow at which Alice Marriott
received her Cheyenne name.

Minnie Cross. She and Robert had been married in a double-wedding ceremony with Mary and Jim Inkanish.

War dancing before Mary's give-away and Alice's naming ceremony.

*Mary, center, and Alice, second from right, at the give-away before
Alice received her Cheyenne name.*

*Mary's friend John Fletcher, accompanied by a younger man,
dancing the "Honor Dance" at Alice's naming ceremony.*

Mary Little Bear Inkanish, holding a child's buckskin dress, 1961.

That was on Friday. In the afternoon, Mama seated herself on the east side of the lodge, near the drummers. Soon she began to sing with them, and before the day was over she was leading the singing; singing old, old Sun Dance songs many of the younger people had never heard, for the men who had made them were gone, and only a few people of the generation that knew those songs and singers were left. Mr. Cone produced a tape recorder, and with the permission of the priests made recordings of them. Carol moved happily about with her camera, and Father Powell and Alice watched and took notes. Nobody objected; for the time being, they were Mama's family, and could do as they liked.

Mama was quiet that evening. She was too full to eat supper— in fact, none of them had much appetite. In the evening, the men returned to the dance.

"You want to go with them?" Mama asked.

"I think I'll type up my notes and go to bed," Alice replied. "What about you, Carol?"

"I'm tired, too," Carol decided. "You can't take pictures at night very well." She unlocked the door of the room she and Alice shared.

"Ahneece," Mama whispered, "you remember that little red wine we drink in San Francisco?"

"Yes. Why?"

"I wish I had some now. My stomach is tired; might make me feel sleepy."

Obediently Alice crossed the highway to the liquor store, bought a half pint of port, and returned.

"How long have you felt this way?" she inquired.

"Oh, since last winter. Not all the time; just sometimes. Then Joe get me little red wine and I feel better and go to sleep."

"I'm worried about Mama," Alice told Carol when she entered their room. "I don't understand why she should suddenly turn into a wino."

"Oh, she hasn't," Carol answered practically. "She's old and tired, and she's eaten more in one day than she has in years. A little wine won't hurt her. My grandmother always said it was the best thing for you when you're tired—except for gin."

And in the morning, Mama indeed seemed all right, and they spent Saturday at the Sun Dance as they had the previous day. They all went to bed early, because they had to be up at daylight for Father Powell's naming ceremony.

When Alice tapped on Mama's door next morning, Mama roused, but decided to go back to sleep instead of getting up. The naming at sunrise was very beautiful, and when it was over, Alice asked John Stands In Timber what the name meant.

"Stone Forehead," John translated. "He was big man once. Great honor to be named for him, Father."

"I'm going to celebrate a Mass of thanksgiving," Father Powell said. "Alice, I know you'll join me. Will any of the rest of you?"

"Yes, if you'll do it at eleven, instead of five in the morning," answered Carol. "I'm not Anglican and I'm hungry. Alice is, too. We'll get something to eat and you can have your Mass at a civilized hour."

"There is the new four-hour rule, Father," Alice reminded him." Since it is only six-thirty I will be able to take Communion by eleven."

So Father Powell reluctantly gave in and returned to the motel, while the others ate scrambled eggs and coffee at Brownie's and returned to nap until ten-thirty.

Mama came out of her room as Alice entered Father Powell's. "What's she doing in there with him?" Mama asked suspiciously.

"He's going to say Mass," Carol replied.

"Why don't you go?"

"It's not my religion. Besides, I thought you wanted to go to the Sun Dance, so I offered to take you."

"You take me to get hot cakes, too?"

"Surely, if you want them."

Another thought occurred to Mama as she settled herself in the car. "Where's Mr. Cones? That's his religion."

"I guess he's being all Cheyenne today. He stayed at the camp, at John Hill's tent."

A little pause, as they turned into Main Street. "I used to pray like that, when I was a schoolgirl at Colony."

"Would you like to go back and pray with them now?"

"I be too ashamed."

"Why?"

"I just can pray in Cheyenne now. I forget them English words."

Carol stopped the car before Brownie's restaurant. "Look, Mama. God is great, and He understands people's hearts, not just their words. We'll go back. They can pray in English, and you can pray in Cheyenne, and I'll pray in Hebrew." And she spun the car in the middle of the deserted street and drove the two blocks back to the motel.

"You buy me hot cakes afterwards?" Mama asked.

"Yes, I'll buy you hot cakes."

They entered Father Powell's room without knocking. The bed had been neatly made up, and a cattle-brand blanket was hung over the mirror above the dressing-table, which served as an altar. Alice, a white cambric handkerchief over her hair, knelt beside the bed, perspiration streaming down her face and neck. In a chair by the altar, half-hidden by the opened door, sat John Stands In Timber. His head was tipped back and the chair supported his broad hat; his legs were outstretched and he was snoring wholeheartedly. Father Powell stopped the service and politely stepped into the bathroom to allow the newcomers to pass between the large bed and the dressing-table to seat themselves on the bed beside Alice. Then, in alb and amice, he returned to resume the service at the General Confession.

Mama sat very still. Then, almost miraculously, little by little, a few at a time, the English words returned to her, and she joined Alice in the responses. All the way through the service to the Gloria in Excelsis she went, remembering the Reverend Givvens and all the other preachers she had seen and known and watched.

At the end of the service Father Powell again retired to the bathroom, and removed his outer vestments. In his black robe he emerged as his own acolyte, to extinguish the candles. Then he opened the door and they all filed out, politely shaking hands with him as they left.

"Join you at Brownie's," said Father Powell, and took up his last duty of the day, to shake John awake. This was accomplished by removing John's hat—enough to wake any cowman.

"What name they give him?" Mama asked John as they packed into the corner booth.

"Stone Forehead," he told her.

"Stone Bonehead," Mama remarked reflectively. "That's a good name." And as long as she lived, Father Powell remained Stone Bonehead to her.

That was the last day of the dance. In the ring of dancers was a boy, about fifteen years old, and just outside, behind him, sat his sister, who was crippled with polio and had to be in a wheelchair. Their grandparents were friends of John's.

"He pledge for his sister," John informed them. "If he last out the dance, she maybe get well."

"He'll never make it," said Father Powell, experienced with boys.

"He make it," Mama said. "If he go this long, he make it."

As she spoke, the boy swayed, stumbled, and fell. His sponsor caught him up, and laid him on the bed of sage. Then he and the head priest went to work, brushing his body from finger- and toe-tips to the heart, with an eagle wing. They sprinkled him with water, but did not give him any to drink. Slowly, the boy's glazed eyes opened, he shook his head to clear it, and stood up. After a moment, while his sponsor fanned him with the eagle wing, he set his whistle in his mouth and resumed dancing.

"It's a miracle," Father Powell exclaimed.

"A Cheyenne miracle," Mama added. "You make your prayers your way, I make mine Cheyenne way now." She returned to her former place by the drummers, and once more began to sing.

"I think she's right," Father Powell said, watching her. "We've seen two miracles today." Nobody contradicted him.

Late in the afternoon, with the sun low in the west, the dance ended. With his eagle wing fan, the priest drove the dancers out of the lodge. First to the east, then to the south, then to the west, and last to the north. Four times they ran, those tired men, and each time the boy ran with them. When they came out through the north, the boy's father was waiting to catch him in his arms as he took his last staggering steps and carry him away to camp to be tended. The sponsor followed, pushing the little girl's wheelchair.

23

GOOD-BYE, MAMA

We are not going to linger on the next two years. Mama grew steadily weaker, and her English began to fail her more frequently. She still spoke clearly in Cheyenne. Joe, the only one of her children who was left, was constantly with her, trying his best to care for his mother.

He took her to the Indian Hospital in Lawton, to a specialist in Oklahoma City, and back to Anadarko, where he settled her in a nursing home, newly opened and clean, where she could be with people she had known most of her life.

Carol and Alice went with her, and when she was in bed resting, she raised her arm. "When I go, Ahneece," she whispered, "you take these bracelets Dougnas give me. They for you."

"I hope I won't wear them for a long time," Alice said.

"They yours, but I keep them little whiles yet," Mama reminded her, and went to sleep.

On the next visit, a week later, Carol noticed that the bracelets were gone. They were never found, and Mama herself did not miss them. They sat by her bed and fed her ice cream, and Joe waited patiently.

Then, a few weeks later, he called.

"You better come, Alice," he said, and that was all. By the time Carol and Alice reached Anadarko, Mama had left them.

The next day Minnie Big Bear's daughter, Sophie, came with a pair of moccasins, so small they could have been a child's. Carol braided an old-time belt, and Alice combed Mama's hair and painted her face. They made sure she wore an old-time reservation dress, and was wrapped in a shawl. Another shawl was laid over the coffin and at the right time was given to Martha Thomas, last of the members of the Women's Heart Club.

Spencer Ahpeahtone, the Kiowa Methodist minister, read the service and preached a brief sermon. Then they all drove to the sunny hillside, and left her there with Jim and Josephine, to rest at last.

As Spencer said that day, "Mama, in heaven there are no good-byes."

SELECTED BIBLIOGRAPHY

Dorsey, George A. *The Cheyennes:* Part II, *The Sun Dance.* Chicago: Field Colum-
bian Museum, Publication No. 103, 1905.

Grinnell, George Bird. *The Fighting Cheyennes.* Norman, Okla.: University of
Oklahoma Press, 1956.

———. *The Cheyenne Indians: Their History and Ways of Life.* 2 vols. Introduction
by Mari Sandoz. New York: Cooper Square Publishers, 1962.

Hoebel, E. Adamson. *The Cheyennes: Indians of the Great Plains.* New York: Holt,
Rinehart & Winston, 1960.

Hoig, Stan. *The Sand Creek Massacre.* Norman, Okla.: University of Oklahoma
Press, 1961.

Llewellyn, K. N., and Hoebel, E. Adamson. *The Cheyenne Way: Conflict and Case
Law in Primitive Jurisprudence.* Norman, Okla.: University of Oklahoma
Press, 1941.

Marriott, Alice. *The Crafts Guild of the Cheyenne Women.* Norman, Okla.: Oklahoma Anthropological Association, 1950.

Marriott, Alice, and Rachlin, Carol K. *American Indian Mythology.* New York:
Thomas Y. Crowell Co., 1968.

———. *Peyote—An Account of the Origins and Growth of the Peyote Religion.* New
York: Thomas Y. Crowell Co., 1971.

———. *Plains Indian Mythology.* New York: Thomas Y. Crowell Co., 1975.

Powell, Peter John. *Sweet Medicine: The Continuing Role of the Sacred Arrows, the
Sun Dance, and the Sacred Buffalo Hat in Northern Cheyenne History.* 2 vols.
Norman, Okla.: University of Oklahoma Press, 1969.

Seger, John H. *Early Days Among the Cheyenne and Arapaho Indians.* Edited by
Stanley Vestal. Norman, Okla.: University of Oklahoma Press, 1956.

Stands in Timber, John, and Liberty, Margot. *Cheyenne Memories.* New Haven:
Yale University Press, 1967.

Photo Credits
Margaret LeFranc: frontispiece.
Western History Collections, University of
Oklahoma Library: 25 (both), 26 (both),
27 (both), 89.
Carol Cussen Hampton (Mrs. James
Hampton) Collection: 91, 95.
Carol K. Rachlin: 181, 182 (all), 183,
184 (all), 185, 186 (both), 187 (all), 188,
216 (all), 217, 218 (both), 219.
Clark Inkanish: 90, 91 (both), 92 (both),
93 (all), 94 (all), 95, 96, 213, 214 (all),
215 (both), 220.

INDEX